California's War Against Donald Trump

California's War Against Donald Trump

WHO WINS? WHO LOSES?

• • •

James V. Lacy

Author of the Politico.com Best Seller

Taxifornia: Liberals' Laboratory to Bankrupt America

and

Katy Grimes

Investigative Political Journalist

Cover photo by James V. Lacy

Copyright © 2017 James V. Lacy
All rights reserved, including the right to reproduce this book or portions thereof in any form.
Published by Landslide Communications, Inc., Laguna Niguel, California
ISBN-13: 9781543112726
ISBN-10: 1543112722

Library of Congress Control Number: 2017912078
CreateSpace Independent Publishing Platform
North Charleston, South Carolina
Laguna Niguel, CA

Politics is war without bloodshed
while war is politics with bloodshed.

—Mao Zedong

Contents

Introduction

● ● ●

"CALIFORNIA, IN MANY WAYS, IS out of control," said President Donald Trump, just a month into his presidency.[1] As two authors, both native Californians, one based in the north of the state and the other in the south, who have observed, written, and commented extensively over the years about our state and its public policy, we completely agree with Trump. California is out of control.

California may be the "sixth-largest economy in the world," as its liberal Democrat leaders in control often say, but its wealth creation that gets it to six, which includes agriculture and entertainment, is largely the work of just one industry: Silicon Valley high technology. At the same time, the state has the highest poverty rate in the nation when cost of living is considered, a fact the liberals in control don't like to discuss. Violent crime in major cities is on the rise. Underemployment and unemployment rates regularly exceed those in the rest of the nation.

The state may have the best wine in the nation, yet among the worst schools as well,[2] even though about 40 percent of state funding, the biggest budget line-item by far, out of California's huge $183 billion budget, goes to the schools.[3] It is a state where cities have gone bankrupt, and the state pension system is underfunded by close to $1 trillion. There are over 625,000 public employees drawing pensions across the state, and well over 20,000 of them receive $100,000 or more in annual benefit, but their grossly underfunded pension plans still draw billions of dollars in taxpayer funds previously used for public safety, such as road maintenance, firefighters, and police services, which are all suffering and themselves in need of more funding.

California taxpayers pay the highest state income tax in the nation, the highest state sales tax, the highest gas taxes, and the highest state corporate tax west of the Mississippi. These sky-high taxes yield the state about $150 billion a year, and that is on top of the additional $100 billion Californians pay in local taxes.[4] The tax base is grossly uneven in the state. "Those in the top brackets, a tiny portion of the overall population, pay about half of the state income taxes, which can be a problem," wrote *Sacramento Bee* columnist Dan Walters.[5] The state has been listed almost every year for close to a decade as the worst state in the nation for locating a business by *CEO* magazine.[6]

In a state that is plagued by natural disasters such as wildfires and drought, because of environmentalist objections, a new dam to store sorely needed additional water has not been built since 1959.

Yet with all its problems, California's liberal leaders have decided that rather than work on fixing their own state, it is more important to declare war on Donald Trump and almost all his policies. From sanctuary-city policies to "The Wall," health care, education, the temporary travel ban, federal regulatory policy, thwarting enforcement of immigration laws, and especially climate change, these liberal Democrats in the state are demonstrating such a vicious hostility to Washington, DC, that one wonders if they have even considered if their actions might be doing more harm than good for their causes and the people of the state.

This work takes a thorough, analytical look at how California's war against Donald Trump is faring and reveals just who is winning—and losing—from all the political grandstanding. With hundreds of sources cited, we hope the reader may be persuaded to understand that the state we love and have no plans on leaving, which is facing enormous challenges, is not helped much at all by its liberal leaders' gratuitous resentment toward and lack of willingness to work with the Trump administration in civil fashion, for the benefit of the people. If we cannot persuade, we hope that in this work we have at least offered the reader some intelligent balance in the debate about the future of California.

James V. Lacy
Katy Grimes
September 2017

The Players

● ● ●

CALIFORNIA'S WAR ON DONALD TRUMP involves a wide range of policy makers and elected officials who are "soldiers and generals" in the ongoing political and legal battles and disputes both for and against Trump's policies in the state. As we begin our book, here is a rundown of the major players at war.

1. PRESIDENT DONALD J. TRUMP

On November 8, 2016, the American voters delivered a historic victory to outlier and insurgent Republican, New York real estate mogul, and novice candidate for public office Donald J. Trump. Trump won in thirty of the fifty states, delivering him an electoral college landslide, and won in more counties nationwide than any Republican candidate since Ronald Reagan.[7] In doing so, millions of voters across the nation, fed up with business-as-usual in Washington, DC, could feel as if they took the country back in a "stunning repudiation" of establishment politicians.[8] Trump's victory was the result of his movement to put "America First" once again, to save and reboot the American economy, and to restore America, as Ronald Reagan once said, as a "shining city on the hill." "Make America Great Again" was and still is the Trump motto.

However, for California, the election results told a completely different story. Golden State voters overwhelmingly voted for Trump's Democrat opponent, former secretary of state Hillary Clinton, by a whopping 4.3 million more votes than Trump.[9] Although Clinton's lead in the popular vote topped 2.8 million across the country, the margin was entirely due to the lopsided vote she received in California.[10] California was Trump's poorest showing and the only state in the nation where Hillary Clinton defied the polls. However, the popular vote total *outside California* shows a very different result, with Trump receiving 58,474,401 votes and Clinton obtaining 57,064,530 votes, producing a 1.4-million-vote edge for Trump in the rest of the nation.[11] In this regard, the results of the presidential election in the nation stand in obvious and stark contrast to the results in California. It was as if California and the rest of the nation were simply disconnected on their choices for president.

TRUMP'S NATIONAL AGENDA

Trump's election had everything to do with his ability to win the hearts and minds of voters in key states other than California, winning in similarly "deep blue" states that usually voted for Democrats in previous elections, including Wisconsin, Pennsylvania, West Virginia, and Michigan and the important swing states of Ohio and Florida. Many of his main issues and themes were different and unique from past Republican candidates. Whereas four years earlier Mitt Romney's losing campaign against President Obama had empha-sized more traditional Republican issues of tax reform and spending, gun rights, antiabortion, support for the Iraq War, and criticism of Obamacare,[12] Trump expanded beyond these issues in forcefully speaking out about loss of manufacturing jobs, terrorism, and immigration and its related issues of crime, sanctuary cities, and the failure of the nation to control its borders.

His "top-ten" issues while campaigning, according to PolitiFact,[13] were the following:

1. "Build a wall" and make Mexico pay for it.
2. Temporarily ban Muslims from entering the United States.
3. Bring manufacturing jobs back to the United States.
4. Impose tariffs on unfair trading partners.
5. Renegotiate or withdraw from the North American Free Trade Agreement and Trans-Pacific Partnership.
6. Repeal and replace Obamacare.
7. Renegotiate the Iran deal.

8. Leave Social Security as is.
9. Cut taxes.
10. Destroy ISIS.

Trump also was a critic of China not only on trade policy but also environmental policy issues, as China is a big polluter, saying, "Climate change is just a very, very expensive form of tax." President Trump said, "I often joke that this is done for the benefit of—obviously I joke—but this is done for the benefit of China."[14]

President Trump wasted no time following the inauguration, and he immediately went to work. He signed 13 Congressional Review Act resolutions in his first one hundred days, reversing Obama-era regulations and blocking agencies from reissuing them.[15] "So far the Trump administration is a welcome improvement, rolling back more regulations than any President in history," the *Wall Street Journal* editorial board reported.[16] He also signed thirty executive orders during his first one hundred days, largely unraveling predecessor Barack Obama's policies.[17] A few of the most impactful early executive orders and presidential memorandums included the following:[18]

- March 28: Dismantling Obama's climate-change policy
- March 27: Revoking Obama's labor orders
- March 13: Reorganizing the executive branch
- March 6: New travel ban and agency implementation guidance
- February 28: Reviewing the "Waters of the United States" rule
- February 24: Enforcing regulatory reform
- February 9: Reducing crime
- February 9: Protecting law enforcement

Although he met fierce resistance among congressional Democrats on his plans to reform health care, and in the courts on efforts to establish a temporary travel ban, three big achievements of the Trump administration in its first one hundred days, according to *Time* magazine, were appointing, and subsequently seeing confirmed, forty-nine-year-old conservative Neil Gorsuch to the US Supreme Court; withdrawing from the Trans-Pacific Partnership

Agreement, a trade deal that Trump argued would hurt US manufacturing; and rolling back Obama-era regulations.[19]

As to the future, Trump has repeatedly said that he will keep his campaign promises. Pulling the United States out of the Paris climate-change agreement was one of those promises, an action hailed by coal miners in West Virginia, a usually Democrat state in deep political contrast to California, where Trump won 69 percent of the vote.[20] West Virginians have reason to be pleased with Trump's promises and performance. But what about California?

THE CALIFORNIA "RESISTANCE"

Trump's election set in motion a firestorm in the Democrat supermajority-controlled California. For example, following Trump's announcement that he would refocus climate-change research conducted by the National Aeronautics and Space Administration (NASA) as part of his fight against climate-alarmist policies, California Governor Jerry Brown launched into an epic monologue on the dangers of climate change, and he even threatened to launch California-funded satellites.[21] California Lt. Governor Gavin Newsom, Brown's presumptive heir apparent, threatened Trump's plans for a wall on our southern border with environmental lawsuits.[22] And thousands began demonstrating against Trump and his policies, and his congressional allies in the state, terming their actions a "Trump resistance."[23]

The coming years will surely reveal whether Californians will benefit, or be the losers, in the conflict between the Trump administration's policies and the policy alternatives offered by the liberal Democrats who run California. Following is a rundown on the elected officials and others leading the California "resistance" and some California officials Trump may try to rely on to see his agenda implemented in Washington, DC.

2. GOVERNOR JERRY BROWN

Following Trump's election, California's Democrat Governor Jerry Brown has taken a mostly defiant stance, telling Trump that "California is not turning back" in reference to the president's border security and immigration policies.[24]

Brown, now seventy-nine, even warned the president, "You don't want to mess with California," in an interview on NBC's *Meet the Press* in March.[25] "We're not going to sit around and just play patsy and say 'Hey, go ahead. Lock us in. Do whatever the hell you want. Deport 2 billion, 2 million people,'" Brown said to NBC host Chuck Todd. "No. We're going to fight, and we're going to fight very hard. But we're not going to bring stupid lawsuits or be running to the courthouse every day. We're going to be careful."[26]

Brown's bravado on national TV, however, was very different from his attitude just the month before, when he went to Washington, DC, with his hat in hand to ask the administration for emergency federal assistance in responding to the overflow spillway break at the Oroville Dam in Northern California, which threatened to flood the surrounding communities all the way down to Sacramento.[27] Brown got his assistance from the Trump administration, regardless of the political theater on *Meet the Press*.

BROWN'S FREUDIAN COMPETITION

Jerry Brown comes from a deeply political family. His father, Edmund G. "Pat" Brown, started out as the San Francisco district attorney before being elected attorney general in 1950.[28] He went on to serve two terms as governor, including his notable defeat of Richard Nixon on his way to reelection in 1962. Pat Brown was known as the "Architect of the Golden State."[29] As governor from 1959–1967, the senior Brown built most of the state's infrastructure, expanded the state's highways and freeway network, and began the State Water Project. The State Water Project includes the California Aqueduct, canals, and pump stations, which helped to establish fertile agricultural lands in the central valley. Pat Brown lost a third bid for governor to Ronald Reagan[30] by over a million votes.

Jerry Brown was elected California governor in 1974 and again in 1978. But his two terms were not without actions in favor of public employees that would set the stage for further problems in the state. "Arguably Brown's biggest mistake was signing legislation in 1978 that allowed collective bargaining for public employee unions," Demographer Joel Kotkin wrote.[31] "This opened the door for a power grab that eventually drove the state toward semi-permanent penury. Brown's early embrace of environmentalism also set a pattern of state green engineering that, although clearly avant-garde, also tipped the state's competitive edge." In fact, the Brown administration was not successful on many policy issues, and he found himself rebuked by voters. In 1978, over Jerry Brown's opposition, voters passed Proposition 13, which halted skyrocketing property taxes and imposed a two-thirds vote on passage of all future tax increases.[32]

In a further rebuke, in 1986, four years after Brown left the governor's office, voters ousted three of Jerry Brown's controversial state Supreme Court justices in a landslide vote, 67 to 33 percent.[33] Republicans followed Brown in the governorship for the next sixteen years: George Deukmejian, elected in 1982 and 1986, and Pete Wilson, elected in 1990 and 1994.

Brown's In-Between Years

Jerry would eventually return to the governor's mansion in 2010. Prior to his third term, there were thirty-two years in between that reveal an "all-over-the-map" history for Brown. After two terms as governor from 1975 to 1983 and losing a race for US Senate, Brown ducked out of public life and traveled to Japan to study Zen Buddhism.[34] He took a seven-year sabbatical, traveling to Mexico, practicing Zen Buddhism in Japan, and visiting India, where he worked with Mother Theresa.

After returning, in 1989 Brown ran for and was elected chairman of the California Democratic Party. He resigned in 1991 and sought the party's presidential nomination the following year, losing to Bill Clinton.[35]

Brown ran for president in 1976, 1980, and 1992.[36] From the mid-1990s, Brown lived in a warehouse building in Oakland and ran a political organization called "We the People," aimed at education and sustainable food production. Brown had a daily radio program, also called "We the People," in which he shared many of his liberal and sometimes "offbeat" ideas. Interestingly, many of the broadcasts have been taken down from the radio's website.[37]

In 1998, Brown launched a successful mayoral campaign and served two terms as mayor of Oakland. Sadly, during Brown's term crime was rampant, and homicides and violent crime spiked.[38] In fact, during and after eight years of Brown serving as mayor, Oakland continued to be on the list of the top-ten most dangerous cities in the nation compiled by the Federal Bureau of Investigation (FBI).[39]

By 2006, Brown reentered state politics and ran for state attorney general. "Mayor" Brown's bid to become California's top cop was successful, regardless of Oakland's high murder rate. In the year he was elected attorney general, there had already been a record 145 killings in Oakland.[40] Jerry's tenure as California attorney general was marred by scandals. In 2009, it was reported by *McClatchy News Bureau* that while Brown's office was issuing subpoenas in a large probe of public pension fund corruption, his campaign received $52,500 in contributions from relatives and a company of the two California businessmen he was investigating.[41]

In 2010, Brown was named the nation's worst state attorney general in America by the Competitive Enterprise Institute (CEI). "One of the most fundamental duties of a state attorney general is to defend all state laws against constitutional challenges. As Attorney General, Brown has abdicated that duty by picking and choosing which laws to defend, and even seeking to undermine those he disagreed with (regardless of their constitutionality)" CEI reported. The criteria categories for being named the worst attorney general in America include the following: ethical breaches and selective applications of the law, fabricating law, usurping legislative powers, and predatory practices. Brown received an F grade from CEI in each area.[42]

CEI also criticized Brown for his alleged attacks on the California Constitution, including a provision that had been upheld by the federal courts more than a decade earlier: Article 1, Section 31 of the California Constitution bars California's government from imposing racial or gender preferences, including race-based affirmative action. It was adopted by California voters in 1996 as Proposition 209 and was upheld in 1997 by a federal appeals court. In 2009, Brown told the California Supreme Court to ignore this provision because, he claimed, it was unconstitutional.[43]

In his January 2015 State of the State address, Brown said he wanted the entire state of California, rich in oil and natural gas, to reduce petroleum consumption by 50 percent, have 50 percent of electricity come from renewable sources, and increase energy efficiency in all existing buildings by 50 percent—all within 15 years, by the year 2030.[44]

But Brown expanded his themes in his January 2017 State of the State address to make it very clear that he would be at odds with the Trump administration and the president. Brown dug in his heels and pledged to continue forging dubious climate agreements with other states and countries. Brown defended the Affordable Care Act and hinted at California creating its own single-payer health-care system, and he vowed to continue California's sanctuary policies for illegal aliens.[45]

During his address, only four days after President Trump's first speech to a joint session of Congress, rather than focusing on what ails the Golden State, most of Brown's speech revolved around how he would grapple with the new Republican president. "California is not turning back—not now, not ever," Brown defiantly declared. "The recent election and inauguration of a new president have shown deep divisions across America," Brown said. "While no one knows what the new leaders will actually do, there are signs that are disturbing. We have seen the bald assertion of 'alternative facts.' We have heard the blatant attacks on science."[46]

Despite campaign promises, together with those of the state's Democrats, to balance the state budget, after so many tax increases, the budget remains out of balance because of an apparent incapacity to control spending. Brown's 2011 state budget was $85 billion; his 2017 budget grew to more than $122 billion, and his 2018 budget is a record $183 billion. None of Brown's budgets address the state's staggering unfunded pension and retiree health-care liabilities or the state's overall debt from borrowing.[47] In his fairy-tale budgets fraught with accounting gimmicks, such as "borrowing" money from numerous special funds specifically earmarked for other uses, Brown has perpetuated California's profligate spending without restraint.[48]

HIGH-SPEED-RAIL BOONDOGGLE

An important "legacy" project to consider in brewing conflict between Washington, DC, and Sacramento is Brown's high-speed-rail project. While

California's once-beautiful highways and roads crumble and decay, Brown has been pushing a high-speed-rail system linking Northern and Southern California. The cost will be well over $100 billion regardless of its modified $68 billion price tag.[49] President Trump and California's Republican congressional delegation want to end federal funding for the high-speed rail. "Time and again, the high-speed rail boondoggle has proven to be an unfeasible project that will put undue and damaging pressure on our state budget, ultimately hurting taxpayers," House Majority Leader Kevin McCarthy said in a statement in 2014 slamming Brown and state lawmakers for including hundreds of millions of dollars in the state budget for the dubious high-speed-rail project.[50]

Another train project—the electrification a Caltrain line between San Jose and San Francisco—may have to wait until an audit can be done of Brown's high-speed-rail project. The $650 million federal grant for the electrification of the San Francisco Bay Area train system was initially suspended by US Transportation Secretary Elaine Chao at the behest of McCarthy, but she eventually approved the grant, an action of the Trump administration that one would think Brown would appreciate.[51]

3. SENATE PRESIDENT PRO TEMPORE KEVIN DE LEÓN, D-LOS ANGELES

California Senate President Pro Tempore Kevin de León, D-Los Angeles, is a former community organizer for the powerful California Teachers Association, a union man with no real private-sector work history.[52] De León grew up in a poor Latino community in San Diego. His father was a cook of Chinese descent, and his mother was a housekeeper from Guatemala, who moved de León and his two older half sisters back and forth between San Diego and Tijuana, Mexico. Although he was later accepted to the University of California at Santa Barbara, de León dropped out of college.[53] De León, whose real birth name is Kevin León, boasted in February that "half his family" was in the country illegally and using false documents.[54] De León has made supporting illegal immigrants and climate change his causes du jour,[55] putting himself in direct policy conflict with the Trump agenda.

The Climate According to Kevin de León

De León previously authored legislation mandating a target of 50 percent reduction in carbon emissions by 2030.[56] Although emissions have been steadily declining regardless of de León's legislation, and are expected to continue to decline regardless of further regulation (as discussed in detail later in this work), Democrats and de León needed to ramp up their controlling restrictions. So, he's drafting a new plan to make California's electricity sources 100 percent "climate friendly" by 2045.[57]

De León's Sanctuary State Plan

De León has also authored Senate Bill 54, effectively turning California into a sanctuary state by providing cover from federal authorities to illegal aliens, including many who are violent felons.[58] With Trump's threat to withdraw federal funding from sanctuary cities—and states—de León accused the administration and president of "white supremacy." "It has become abundantly clear that Atty. Gen. [Jeff] Sessions and the Trump administration are basing their law enforcement policies on principles of white supremacy—not American values," de León said in a statement in April. "Their constant and systematic targeting of diverse cities and states goes beyond constitutional norms and will be challenged at every level."[59]

California Senate Democrats under de León also proposed a bill to prevent the Trump administration from building a wall along the California–Mexico border, without prior approval of California voters, claiming the border wall would "threaten endangered species and sensitive habitats."[60] However, Democrats are being disingenuous; there are already many miles of multilayered border fencing between Mexico and California, and the fencing was authorized and built during the presidencies of Bill Clinton and Barack Obama.

4. State Attorney General Xavier Becerra

Xavier Becerra says that opposing Donald Trump's policies is "a team sport."[61] He has been called the "leader of the California resistance" by the *San*

Francisco Chronicle.[62] Following the November election, Governor Brown appointed Rep. Xavier Becerra, D-Los Angeles, to replace State Attorney General Kamala Harris, who won election to the seat vacated by the retiring US Senator Barbara Boxer.[63] The *Chronicle* says he was chosen by Brown because it was "widely accepted" that he "would have the gravitas and savvy to defend California values in a hostile environment."[64]

Becerra had served in Congress since 1992. As chairman of the House Democrat Caucus, Becerra was the highest-ranking Latino in Congress, and his appointment made him the state's first Latino attorney general.[65] A Stanford Law School graduate, before his appointment as state attorney general, Becerra had just three years' experience working in the Civil Division of the Attorney General's Office, some thirty years ago, before he entered Congress.[66]

Becerra is not just a Democrat; he is a very liberal Democrat. In fact, he has welcomed the endorsements and support of Far Left groups such as the Democratic Socialists of America, which formally endorsed his reelection to the House in 1996, and is supported by other Far Left groups including the Chicano Coalition for Peace and Social Justice and Latinos for Peace, an anti–Iraq War front group with radical connections.[67]

California State Assemblyman Reggie Jones-Sawyer, D-Paramount, opened Becerra's confirmation hearing by praising the idea of a "legal war" between California and President Trump after accusing Trump of running "the most xenophobic campaign in modern history."[68] Becerra even opened a Washington, DC, office "to communicate more closely with his former House colleagues and the Trump administration," Becerra explained in a May news conference. "I think it's extremely useful to have eyes and ears in Washington, D.C. It's helpful to continue to have that reach to my former colleagues, to continue to have someone who can, day to day, secure those types of contacts that we need."[69]

Governor Brown introduced Becerra at his confirmation hearing by warning that "there are big battles ahead." "The appointment of Xavier Becerra as California attorney general, meanwhile, has everything to do with the protection of illegal aliens," Lloyd Billingsley wrote in a *Frontpage* article, which further noted:

Becerra will work well with Jerry Brown, who turned California into a sanctuary state decades ago. As Daniel Greenfield noted, Becerra also blocked funds for the war on Islamic terrorist groups such as Al Qaeda, claiming that he wanted to avoid "another Vietnam." He also voted against a commendation for US troops' service in Iraq. His passion, however, remains the defense of illegals and he is a perfect fit for governor Jerry Brown, uncritical of sanctuary cities that shelter violent criminals.[70]

On his appointment, Becerra promised to resist "federal intrusion" and the immigration policies of the Trump administration, including Trump's "extreme vetting" order blocking immigration from a handful of nations in the Middle East, denouncing the action that activated left-wing protests as "in so many ways unjust and anti-American," as the *Sacramento Bee* reported.[71] "It discriminates against human beings based on their faith. It denies entry to those with proven and legitimate fears of death and persecution. It tramples on centuries of American tradition," Becerra said in a statement in January, following Trump's inauguration.[72]

Leading up to Brown's 2017 May Revise Budget, Becerra asked for more money in his budget to oppose Trump.[73] Brown provided an additional $6 million and thirty-one new positions to help Becerra "address [the] new legal workload" involved in fighting Trump and his administration.[74]

In April on ABC's *This Week*, Becerra said President Trump's proposed wall on the US–Mexico border was "medieval."

"I'm still trying to figure out who believes a medieval situation to fix the immigrant situation is what we need," Becerra said.[75] "One, Donald Trump is reneging on his promise to have someone else pay. I think American taxpayers are very much aligned with Mexico. None of them, not the taxpayers or Mexico wants to pay for a medieval wall."[76]

5. US Senator Dianne Feinstein

Democrat Dianne Feinstein has served in the US Senate since 1992. Prior to running for Senate, Feinstein won election to San Francisco's Board of

Supervisors in 1969 and served on the board through the 1970s. She served as the thirty-eighth mayor of San Francisco from 1978 to 1988—but only after running for mayor twice, losing to Joseph Alioto in 1971, and finishing a distant third to George Moscone in the 1975 election. Former San Francisco supervisor Dan White fatally shot Mayor Moscone and Supervisor Harvey Milk in November 1978, forcing Feinstein into the position of acting mayor. A month later, she was selected to serve out the balance of Moscone's term.[77]

In 1990 Feinstein ran for governor of California against Republican Pete Wilson. Her campaign was well funded by her third husband, investment banker Richard Blum, but she lost to Wilson. In early 1991, Feinstein announced she would run for Wilson's former Senate seat in the 1992 election, which she won.[78] During her term of office, she had been accused of authoring legislation to benefit her husband, who is a University of California regent, and his business interests.[79,80,81] "In 2013, a construction group partially owned by Blum's investment firm scored a construction contract for California's high-speed rail project valued at $985,142,530," Breitbart reported. "Blum's company, CBRE, was selected in March 2011 as the sole real estate agent on sales expected to fetch $19 billion," the *New York Post* reported. Most voters didn't notice that Blum is a member of CBRE's board and served as chairman from 2001 to 2014."[82]

Feinstein turned eighty-three in 2017, and there have been questions about her retiring. At a town-hall meeting, she was asked how she feels about term limits for senators. Feinstein said she doesn't believe term limits should be set, and she wouldn't commit on plans to seek reelection.[83]

Judiciary Committee Ranking Member

As the top Democrat on the powerful Senate Judiciary Committee, Feinstein will have a say on every single one of the Trump administration's judicial appointments. At the same time, Feinstein is under "scalding anti-Trump fervor" from liberal Democrat activists in the state who want her to take the hardest possible line against the president.[84] There is little doubt that Feinstein will have some influence on Trump's judicial appointments, which number more than one hundred vacancies nationwide.

Although her opposition to the confirmation of Trump's US Supreme Court nominee Neil Gorsuch failed, nevertheless, because of a Senate Judiciary Committee custom known as "blue-slipping," Feinstein will at a minimum have the ability to veto or greatly slow down new appointments to the federal judicial branch, US attorneys, and seats held by Californians at the liberal Ninth Circuit Court of Appeals. "Blue-slipping" refers to a practice whereby the chairman of the Senate Judiciary Committee sends information on a judicial nominee to the nominee's home-state senators, regardless of whether they are on the Judiciary Committee. Unless both senators signal their approval by returning the slips, the committee will not consider the nomination.[85] As the ranking member, Feinstein is especially "in the catbird seat" to block and influence California-based judicial appointments.[86]

FEINSTEIN BLOCKS WATER PROJECTS

Water is a big issue in California, even more so in the aftermath of the state's historic drought, and especially for agribusiness, environmentalists, and residential users. Feinstein has an attitude about California water, and it is tilted in favor of the environmentalists, to the detriment of agriculture and residential use. In an example of her water bias, Feinstein used her position on the Appropriations Committee to block the Cadiz Valley Water Project, an important water project in Southern California. Located in the Mohave Desert, the Cadiz plan calls for the construction of a forty-three-mile pipeline that would supply water to the Colorado River Aqueduct from the Cadiz property. "When Cadiz attempted to start the project in the early 2000s with their original partner, Metropolitan Water District, Feinstein used policy riders in the fiscal year 2007 spending bill that blocked Cadiz from receiving any funding," Beth Bauman wrote in 2015.[87]

According to the Environmental Impact Report, four hundred thousand people could benefit from the project, which would provide over sixteen million gallons of drinking water.[88] Located on private land, the project would have no impact on national parks, as Feinstein has asserted in opposition. Cadiz has undergone multiple environmental reviews, including a California Environmental Quality Act review that survived court challenges.[89] Feinstein's "opposition has done a disservice to thousands of Californians who will benefit from this public-private partnership—a project which will deliver new, reliable water without any adverse environmental impacts," Cadiz CEO Scott Slater said in a statement. Feinstein was joined by the Obama administration in an administrative ruling blocking the project in 2015.

Feinstein's opposition to this important infrastructure project will be an area of conflict with congressional leaders and the Trump administration. Republican Rep. Tom McClintock and Democrat Rep. Tony Cardenas, along with sixteen other California congressional representatives, joined in writing to President Trump's Interior Secretary Ryan Zinke, asking him to rescind the Obama-era decision and renew the project. "In a March 29 memorandum, Zinke's Interior Department did just that, rescinding the 2015 decision signed by Timothy Spisak, acting assistant director for Bureau of Land Management's Division of Energy, Minerals, and Realty Management," the *Sacramento Bee* reported,[90] further noting he following:

> The Cadiz water project that would deliver 50,000 acre feet of water to parched communities in Southern California. That's enough to meet the annual residential needs of 100,000 families at no public cost. Without Cadiz, all of that water is lost to evaporation...Sen. Feinstein has also been instrumental in blocking Senate consideration of House legislation (H.R. 2898) that would have allowed us this year to capture and store hundreds of thousands of acre feet of winter runoff that was instead lost to the ocean.[91]

6. US SENATOR KAMALA HARRIS

Until November 2016, Democrat Kamala Harris was California's state attorney general. She received national headlines in 2013 when President Obama called Harris the "best-looking" state attorney general.[92] Now a US Senator, Harris has shown herself to be in a war against President Trump. Harris gave a saber-rattling commencement speech at Howard University in 2017, in which she implored students to "fight against the dark new political climate." Harris painted a dystopian picture in her address and told students they should be concerned for the future, making several shrouded references to Trump's policies.[93] Harris encouraged graduates to enter careers where they can fight to uphold "liberal values," championing Black Lives Matter protesters and labor union activists. Channeling class struggle, a dominant part of radical Left thought, Harris said, "You can march for black lives on the street…You can advocate for environmental justice…you can march for workers on a picket line," even noting that students could become activists to fight for "greater diversity in the arts and entertainment," Campus Reform reported.[94]

Harris is being courted by the liberal media as a potential presidential candidate "of color" for 2020—an attempt to keep identity politics alive.[95] But in California politics, Harris first came into public view in 1994 when then–Assembly Speaker Willie Brown provided Harris, known as Brown's "frequent companion," a high-paying appointment to the California Medical Assistance Commission.[96]

"Harris, a former deputy district attorney in Alameda County, was described by several people at the Capitol as Brown's girlfriend," the *Los Angeles Times* reported.[97] "In March, *San Francisco Chronicle* columnist Herb Caen called her 'the Speaker's new steady.'" Harris accepted the appointment after serving only six months as Brown's appointee to the Unemployment Insurance Appeals Board, which paid $97,088 a year.[98]

Soft on Crime

As San Francisco's elected district attorney for six years, Harris was widely criticized by law enforcement[99] for being soft on violent crime and homicides, both of which dramatically increased in San Francisco during her tenure, whereas crime fell statewide, according to California Department of Justice statistics.[100] Harris was frequently described as politically ambitious and cautious and was criticized for doing nothing to take on political corruption.[101]

Juan Francisco Lopez-Sanchez, a felon who had been deported five times, had been serving forty-six months in a Southern California prison but was returned to San Francisco to face a twenty-year-old marijuana charge. On April 15, 2015, San Francisco Sheriff Ross Mirkarimi duly released Lopez-Sanchez. On July 1, 2015, police arrested Lopez-Sanchez in the shooting death of Kathryn

Steinle, thirty-two, on a San Francisco pier.[102] Governor Brown and then–Attorney General Harris both backed up Mirkarimi's decision to release Lopez-Sanchez.[103] The murder of Kate Steinle prompted neither politician to challenge policies that give sanctuary to violent felons after multiple deportations.

The Freshman Senator and CIA Climate Change

During CIA director Mike Pompeo's Senate confirmation hearings in January 2017, Harris grilled him on whether climate change was a leading national security threat. "CIA Director Brennan, who has spent a 25-year career at the CIA as an analyst, a senior manager and station chief in the field, has that when 'CIA analysts look for deeper causes of rising instability in the world, one of the causes those CIA analysts see is the impact of climate change,'" Harris said. "Do you have any reason to doubt the assessment of those CIA analysts?"[104]

Pompeo said the CIA would gather information on all threats to American security, including any that stem from climatic activity, and present them to policy makers. But Harris would not let up. "In the past you have questioned the scientific consensus on climate change," Harris followed up. She began to cite NASA and various other sources saying that at least 97 percent of active climate scientists believe in global warming caused by human activity, the *Washington Examiner* reported.[105] "Do you have any reason to doubt NASA's findings?" she asked. Pompeo defended his positions on climate change and said, "Frankly, as director of CIA, I'd prefer…not to get into the details of climate debate and science…My role is going to be so different and unique from that, it is going to be to work alongside warriors keeping Americans safe."[106] Following the confirmation hearing, Harris said Pompeo's views on global warming called into question his ability to accept evidence and the consensus of the intelligence community.[107]

7. House Minority Leader Nancy Pelosi, D-San Francisco

On Election Night 2016, PBS's Judy Woodruff interviewed House Minority Leader Nancy Pelosi, D-San Francisco, on her prediction of the election outcome. "Well, tonight, I believe that the Democrats will come out in a stronger position," Pelosi said. "We will, of course, retain the White House, with the election of Hillary Clinton. I believe we will gain the United States Senate. It will be close, but we will gain the United States Senate. And we will pick up many seats in the House of Representatives."[108]

Following Trump's win, Pelosi admitted she was blindsided by the loss: "I didn't think Hillary Clinton was going to be elected president—I knew she would be elected president."[109] In March, following the surprising election outcome, Pelosi was on NBC's *Today*, discussing allegations and investigations into Russian meddling in the 2016 election and Trump's win.[110] Host Savannah Guthrie intimated that Trump was being blackmailed by Russia, teeing up a softball for Pelosi to hit out of the park. "Something you say a lot, and have said a lot, is that you think that the Russians have something on President Trump. You say, 'What do they have on him?' Do you actually have information to back up that question or are you just speculating without evidence?" Guthrie asked Pelosi.[111] "No, I just wonder what the Russians have politically, personally, or financially on President Trump," Pelosi answered. "Because this is about a national security issue. Why would the President of the United States just come in and start to flirt with the idea of lifting sanctions on Russia in terms of their behavior in Eastern Europe? Why would the President of the United States question the START treaty? Why would the President of the United States put Putin on a pedestal and diminish the greatness of America in that? There's something wrong with this picture."[112] Pelosi hasn't let up on the Russian interference theme since.

Known as an outstanding fundraiser for the Democratic Party and candidates, Pelosi has been leading House Democrats since 2002.[113] Yet many San Francisco progressives say Pelosi and the aging Democratic National Committee (DNC) core have lost touch, as they remain wedded to their special-interest groups and their own self-interest.[114] With respect to future elections, many progressives express concern that Pelosi and her aging party no longer represent the middle class, working families, or the youth who still love Bernie Sanders. Democrats' current message—besides "the Russians interfered in the 2016 election"—seems like resentment, anger, envy, jealousy, and outright hatred. They're offering little to their voters by way of policy issues.

"You put on your armor in Washington, and we eat nails for breakfast, nails for lunch and nails for dinner," Pelosi is fond of telling caucus members, as reported by *US News*.[115] "By the time 2018 rolls around, when Democrats look for gains in the midterms, there's some feeling that her cache will have ebbed even further, given that she's likely to remain a Republican punching bag," In February, an NBC News/*Wall Street Journal* survey measured her national favorability rating at just 19 percent, trailing House Speaker Paul Ryan by 15 points and Trump by 24 points."[116] "She can't go into rural communities, she can't go into Rust Belt communities. Can Nancy go into your district and help you? The answer is no for two-thirds of our members," a second Democrat congressman said.[117]

8. THREE HOUSE DEMOCRATS: "IMPEACH NOW, THEN INVESTIGATE FURTHER"

REP. MAXINE WATERS, D-LOS ANGELES

Rep. Maxine Waters, D-Los Angeles, represents a heavily black district in Los Angeles. She can't get over the fact that Donald Trump is president and speaks frequently about working to get him impeached.[118] She has led numerous chants at rallies, including "We've got to stop his ass!" and "Impeach forty-five!"[119]

Waters has also "called out" many of Trump's top agency appointees, including Dr. Ben Carson, the Housing and Urban Development (HUD) Secretary, calling him "unqualified," among other things: "Ben Carson was appointed to be the HUD secretary," Waters said.[120] "He knows nothing about the mission of HUD. He doesn't care about people in public housing. He believes that if you are poor, it is your own fault. And he doesn't know the difference between an immigrant and a slave."[121]

Recently Waters suggested that Trump should be dragged down the hall of Congress to his impeachment. "Instead of disabled people in wheelchairs, the only person who should be dragged anywhere is Trump—down the hall, to impeachment," she tweeted, referencing the protesters who were dragged from Senate Majority Leader Mitch McConnell's office while protesting a bill.[122]

Although she can't articulate a constitutionally impeachable offense, Waters, who actually has been caught and named as one of the "Most Corrupt Members of Congress," makes one wonder if her constant sounding of the impeachment drum is egregious political grandstanding or deflection away from her own ethical issues.[123]

REP. BRAD SHERMAN, D-SHERMAN OAKS

In July 2017, Rep. Brad Sherman, D-Sherman Oaks, introduced an article of impeachment against President Trump, accusing the president of obstructing justice during the federal investigation of Russia's 2016 election interference.[124] Sherman's district voted for Hillary Clinton in the presidential election, but he is especially antagonistic, and he has even compared Donald Trump to ISIS, saying both are "bent on destroying civilization."[125]

Sherman alleges in his article of impeachment[126] that Trump's "abrupt firing" of James Comey as FBI director amounts to obstructing justice and "high crimes and misdemeanors," amid the probes of whether Trump's campaign colluded with the Russian government to swing the election, *The Hill* reported.[127] Sherman has one cosponsor in Rep. Al Green, D-Texas, who has called for additional articles of impeachment.[128] In support of impeachment, Sherman wrote to his colleagues in the Congress:

> As the investigations move forward, additional evidence supporting additional Articles of Impeachment may emerge. However, as to Obstruction of Justice and 18 U.S.C. § 1512 (b)(3), the evidence we have is sufficient to move forward now. And the national interest requires that we do so.
>
> I act not for partisan advantage. Having served with Mike Pence in the House for twelve years, I disagree with him on most issues of public policy. But we must move forward as quickly as possible to ensure a competent government that respects the Constitution and the rule of law, even if we end up with a President who is effective and dedicated to regressive policies.[129]

However, Democrat leaders have moved to distance themselves from impeachment as an issue, fearing that it strengthens Trump's political base.[130] On the House floor, Rep. Mike Capuano, D-Massachusetts, stood up to "heavily criticize" Sherman for the impeachment process, and even House Minority Leader Nancy Pelosi agreed.[131]

Rep. Adam Schiff, D-Burbank

Rep. Adam Schiff, D-Burbank, serves as the ranking member of the House Intelligence Committee. He said no one should "rush to embrace the most extraordinary remedy for removing a president."[132] But Schiff is no apologist for Donald Trump, who has been a target of criticism by Schiff repeatedly on the Intelligence Committee.

Despite denials from even the Obama administration's top intelligence officials that there was evidence of collusion between the Russian government and Trump, and a specific denial by James Clapper, Schiff said on *Meet the Press*, "I was surprised to see Director Clapper say that because I don't think you can make that claim categorically as he did. I would characterize it this way at the outset of the investigation: There is circumstantial evidence of collusion. There is direct evidence, I think, of deception and that's where we begin the investigation."[133]

Schiff's press staff has been working overtime to get him in as much media as possible, work that is apparently gaining ground, as evidenced by this comment in a *New Yorker* article: "Appalled by President Trump's muted response to the Russian cyber attack, Adam Schiff has emerged as an unexpected face of Democratic resistance to the new administration."[134]

9. The GOP "Fourteen"

House Majority Leader Kevin McCarthy, R-Bakersfield

Of the fifty-three members of Congress from California, fourteen are Republicans.[135] Following Trump's election, House Majority Leader Kevin McCarthy, R-Bakersfield, was chosen by his House Republican colleagues to remain as the second-highest-ranking leader.[136] Elected to Congress in 2006, McCarthy was first picked for House leadership in 2009 as the Republican's chief deputy whip. He has been majority leader since 2014.

McCarthy served in the California State Assembly from 2002 to 2006, where he served as assembly minority leader from 2004 to 2006.[137] During the House debate and negotiations on the passage of the Obamacare repeal-and-replace bill, McCarthy said Trump called him on the phone and gave him a list of his own Republican members to talk to on collecting votes. "Walk into my office yesterday morning, they say the president's calling again," McCarthy said in an interview. "I know my members well. The president gives me a list of who he thinks it would be best to talk to on the list. And he was right."[138] They all voted for the bill, McCarthy noted.

REP. DEVIN NUNES, R-TULARE

In April, quite surprisingly, House Intelligence Committee Chairman Devin Nunes, R-Tulare, stepped down "temporarily" from his role of leading his committee's investigation into alleged Russian interference in the 2016 presidential campaign, as well as alleged surveillance of Trump associates by the Obama administration.[139] Nunes, who represents California's San Joaquin Valley, was accused of going directly to President Trump with information he alleged showed that the Obama administration asked for the names of Trump transition officials to be improperly unmasked in intelligence reports on foreign nationals.[140] In a statement, Nunes pointed to the extreme efforts of "several leftwing activist groups" to lodge "entirely false and politically motivated" accusations against him with the Office of Congressional Ethics as his reason for stepping aside.[141]

The House Ethics Committee is investigating the allegations against Nunes.[142] He said the "false accusations" against him were timed to distract from reports about the names of Trump associates being "unmasked" in intelligence files during the latter weeks of the Obama administration by former national security adviser Susan Rice.[143]

At a May 2017 Tulare County Lincoln Dinner, Nunes said he stepped aside to protect other vulnerable Republican House members from facing questions about his actions from the media, according to a video of the event published by the *Los Angeles Times*.[144] "The reporters and the national news were going to chase David [Valadao] and every other member of Congress around the country for the next two weeks. Basically what I said, I said, 'Well, screw you,'" Nunes told guests at the Lincoln Club fundraiser. "So I did something that they never thought I would do and I stepped aside, and I gave them a gift."

Nunes said he would return to lead the Russia probe once the ethics charges against him were cleared up. Nunes also said Democrats only want to talk about Russia's election meddling in order to excuse Hillary Clinton's loss to Trump.[145]

REP. DARRELL ISSA, R-VISTA

Rep. Darrell Issa, R-Vista, a member of Congress since 2001, currently is a member of the House Judiciary Committee, the Foreign Affairs Committee, and the Oversight and Government Reform Committee, where he served as the chairman for four years.[146]

The *Los Angeles Times* has reported that Issa is the richest member of Congress, having earned his wealth through development of automobile alarm technologies.[147] A holder of thirty-seven patents himself after a very successful career in business, Issa is currently the chairman of the Judiciary Committee's Subcommittee on Courts, Intellectual Property, and the Internet.

Following Donald Trump's election to the presidency, during an interview with HBO's Bill Maher, Issa was among the first members of Congress to say that a special prosecutor should be brought in to investigate Russia's alleged involvement in the 2016 presidential election, and that Attorney General Jeff Sessions—a friend of Issa's—should recuse himself because he was part of the Trump campaign.[148] Issa is known for his aggressive and thorough investigations into President Barack Obama and Obama's agency officials in Issa's role as chairman of the House Oversight Committee.

A top but failed target of Democrats in the 2016 election, in a district won by Hillary Clinton, Issa won that election by 2,348 votes.[149] He is being targeted again in 2018.[150] Issa has been rather mercilessly protested against by a national Left Wing organization known as "Indivisible"[151] that just isn't satisfied with Issa's calls for an independent Russia probe.

At the California GOP Convention in March 2017, Issa praised Trump during his luncheon speech, but he told reporters afterward, "Donald Trump is not everybody's Republican. He's not everybody's conservative. But he is our president, our president for everybody, and I will agree with him or disagree with him, but I'll try to make him a success."[152]

While Democrats fret over how to win over Rust Belt voters who backed Donald Trump, their chance to win the twenty-four seats they need to win a majority in the US House in next year's midterm election depends on unseating California Republicans like Issa.

REP. DOUG LAMALFA, R-RICHVALE

Rep. Doug LaMalfa, R-Richvale, represents the First Congressional District and serves on the Committee on Natural Resources. A fourth-generation rice farmer and business owner, he runs the Northern California family farming business originally founded by his great-grandfather in 1931.[153]

REP. TOM MCCLINTOCK, R-ELK GROVE

Rep. Tom McClintock, R-Elk Grove, represents the Fourth Congressional District. He is the Chairman of the Water and Power Subcommittee of the House Natural Resources Committee. An outspoken member of the House Budget Committee, McClintock has proposed major fiscal reforms to curb unauthorized appropriations, control mandatory spending, balance the budget, and protect the nation's credit.[154]

REP. PAUL COOK, R-APPLE VALLEY

Rep. Paul Cook, R-Apple Valley, represents the Eighth Congressional District. Col. Paul Cook (ret.), a veteran of the Vietnam War, served twenty-six years in the US Marine Corps. His actions in combat earned him two Purple Hearts and the Bronze Star Medal with a V for valor. He serves on the House Armed Services, Foreign Affairs, and Veterans' Affairs Committees.[155]

REP. JEFF DENHAM, R-TURLOCK

Rep. Jeff Denham, R-Turlock, represents the Tenth Congressional District, which includes all of Stanislaus County and part of San Joaquin County. Denham served in the US Air Force for sixteen years and fought in Operation Desert Storm and Operation Restore Hope in Iraq and Somalia.[156] Democrats put an early target on Denham's Congressional seat in 2018, which he won reelection by less than 5 percent in 2016.

REP. DAVID VALADAO, R-HANFORD

Rep. David Valadao, R-Hanford, represents the Twenty-First Congressional District and serves on the House Committee on Appropriations; he is also the vice chairman of the Subcommittee on Agriculture.[157]

REP. STEVE KNIGHT, R-PALMDALE

Rep. Steve Knight, R-Palmdale, represents the Twenty-Fifth Congressional District and serves on the House Armed Services Committee.[158] Knight is considered among the most vulnerable of Republicans, having won reelection by 6 percent in 2016, while Hillary Clinton carried the district.

REP. ED ROYCE, R-FULLERTON

Rep. Ed Royce, R-Fullerton, is serving his eleventh term in Congress representing the Thirty-Ninth Congressional District, and he serves as the chairman of the Foreign Affairs Committee.[159] Democrats are eager to defeat Royce, who has a significant campaign warchest and has seen little opposition in the past.

Rep. Ken Calvert, R-Corona

Rep. Ken Calvert, R-Corona, represents the Forty-Second Congressional District and serves on the House Appropriations Committee, where he is the chairman of the Interior and the Environment Subcommittee.[160]

Rep. Mimi Walters, R-Irvine

Rep. Mimi Walters, R-Irvine, represents the Forty-Fifth Congressional District and serves on the House Judiciary Committee and the House Committee on Transportation and Infrastructure. Before entering politics, Walters was an investment banker and local elected official.[161] Although Walters represents a district in the heart of the Republican bastion of Orange County, the district has now voted for the Democrat candidate for president in two of the last three national elections, suggesting she may be vulnerable in her reelection campaign.[162]

Rep. Duncan Hunter, R-Alpine

Rep. Duncan Hunter, R-Alpine, represents the Fiftieth Congressional District and serves on the House Armed Services Committee. Following the September 11, 2001, terrorist attacks, Hunter joined the US Marine Corps and served three combat tours overseas in Iraq and Afghanistan.[163]

The Democratic Congressional Campaign Committee announced that it had added Hunter's seat to a long list of targets, in the wake of questions about the spending of his campaign funds on some personal expenses, which Hunter corrected, but the incident led to a federal investigation.[164]

Rep. Dana Rohrabacher, R-Huntington Beach

Rep. Dana Rohrabacher, R-Huntington Beach, represents the Forty-Eighth Congressional District, which stretches along the southern Pacific coastline. Rohrabacher, a former speechwriter for President Ronald Reagan, who has served in the house since 1989, serves as Chairman of the Europe, Eurasia, and Emerging Threats Subcommittee of the House Foreign Affairs Committee.[165]

Politico.com has labeled Rohrabacher as "Putin's favorite Congressman" for some pro-Russian views that Politico says have "made him an outcast."[166]

10. SACRAMENTO MAYOR DARRELL STEINBERG

When President Trump signed his first immigration executive order in January 2017, Sacramento Mayor Darrell Steinberg, a Democrat, called it "an unconscionable threat" to public safety and "a cowardly, reckless and inhumane act" that the city would combat alongside other sanctuary cities.[167] The former Senate president, Steinberg worked as a union lawyer for the California State Employees Association labor union prior to running for public office in 1992. Since then, he's spent all but two years holding political office.[168]

As mayor, Steinberg announced his plans for making homelessness in Sacramento his priority, then vowed to protest President Trump's executive order that temporarily banned citizens from seven Muslim-majority countries from traveling to the United States. "This is a horrible anti-American act by Donald Trump," said Steinberg. "This is against what America stands for."[169] "As mayor of our city, I would never trade away peoples' civil rights for money," Steinberg said. "That's the only place to stand on behalf of this city that turned out 25,000 people to Capitol Mall [for the women's march] and this city that prides itself on its incredible diversity." Steinberg added that his city would "join, if not lead, any effort to fight [the sanctuary city threat] with litigation."[170]

Sacramento has been a sanctuary city since 1985, but with Trump's election, Steinberg and city leaders have ramped up pro–sanctuary city promises. President Trump issued a warning to California after Democrat lawmakers in the state advanced legislation to make it a sanctuary state. In a February interview with Fox News' Bill O'Reilly, Trump threatened to withhold federal funds from "out-of-control" California if it makes good on its promise to become a sanctuary state.[171]

The Sacramento City Council voted unanimously in May 2017 to allot $300,000 of taxpayer money to provide legal services to illegal aliens under the threat of deportation by immigration authorities under President Trump.[172] As for making Sacramento's homeless his priority, that's not working, either.

Homelessness in Sacramento continues to grow.[173] With Sacramento's opulent new $556.6 million downtown Golden One Center basketball arena, the persistent problem of homeless people in the same area raises now-escalating issues of vandalism and theft of local businesses, serious sanitation problems, public intoxication, and crime since Steinberg introduced a "warming center" for the homeless.[174] Compassion may have its limits for the general population in Sacramento. The owner of a floral shop in the area told the *Sacramento Bee*, "I have to step over human feces every day. I have to step over people to get into my business. It's not a good feeling."[175]

11. San Francisco Mayor Ed Lee

In his January State of the City address, San Francisco Mayor Ed Lee reinforced his city's sanctuary-city commitment, despite President Trump's executive order to eliminate funding to sanctuary cities.[176] "We are a sanctuary city now, tomorrow, forever," Lee said. Days later, Mayor Lee and San Francisco City Attorney Dennis Herrera filed a lawsuit against President Trump over the executive order, claiming, "it is not only unconstitutional, it is un-American."

"Under the City's sanctuary policies, Sheriff Vicki Hennessy has ignored 41 requests in the past six months from U.S. Immigration and Customs Enforcement to be notified in advance when undocumented inmates are released," the *San Francisco Examiner* reported.[177]

San Francisco "receives $1.2 billion, 13 percent of its total annual budget, in federal funds, according to City Controller Ben Rosenfield, of which $800 million 'is for federal entitlement programs, including food stamps, foster care, childcare, and Medicaid healthcare funds.' About $200 million is 'an assortment of various grants for a host of smaller programs.'"[178]

In his executive order, Trump said sanctuary policies make cities unsafe. "We are going to get the bad ones out, the criminals and drug dealers and gangsters and gang leaders," Trump said. "The day is over when they can stay in our country and wreak havoc."[179] Yet, San Francisco city officials say sanctuary policies make cities safer and stronger economically by fostering trust in immigrant communities where those are not fearful of deportation if they report crimes, send their children to school, or access other city services.[180] San Francisco houses thirty-eight thousand illegal aliens, yet it receives $509 million from the federal government—nearly the same amount as Los Angeles.[181]

12. LOS ANGELES MAYOR ERIC GARCETTI

An outspoken critic of Donald Trump throughout the campaign, Los Angeles Mayor Eric Garcetti is now trying to figure out how to keep LA's sanctuary-city status without losing the $502 million Los Angeles gets from the federal government.[182] As with the mayors of San Francisco and Sacramento, Garcetti doubled down on sanctuary-city protections for immigrants and released Los Angeles Executive Directive 20, which prohibits city employees and city funding from being used in service of federal immigration enforcement, except when required by law.

According to *Open the Books*, Los Angeles is home to 893,000 illegal aliens—the most in the entire country. But Los Angeles receives the least amount of federal funding per individual—only $126 per resident, $504 per family of four, or $502.5 million total.[183] Approximately eleven million illegal entrants reside within the United States; 20 percent of them live in just twelve American cities, with one of those being Los Angeles.[184]

Garcetti has also asked that US Immigration and Customs Enforcement ("ICE") agents stop identifying themselves as "police" to immigrants, despite the fact that they wear protective vests during operations that often say both "ICE" and "Police" on them. In a letter[185] to David Marin of the Los Angeles division of ICE, Garcetti said that when ICE agents identify themselves as police, they are creating animosity between undocumented immigrants and the Los Angeles Police Department (LAPD).[186] The practice threatens to erode trust between the LAPD and immigrant communities, the mayor claims.

But Garcetti has other worries with his city's sanctuary-city status: Los Angeles submitted its final bid to host the 2024 Summer Olympics, but some are concerned. President Trump said he will stand by his executive order restricting travel from now six majority-Muslim countries, even if it puts LA's Olympic bid at risk, KQED reported.[187]

13. Almost Player: San Diego Mayor Kevin Faulconer

Elected mayor of San Diego in 2014, Kevin Faulconer is an odd duck—a Republican in charge of the eighth-largest city in the United States and the second-largest city in California. A graduate of San Diego State University and a former public relations executive, Faulconer campaigned against alcohol on San Diego's beautiful beaches and served on the City Council before being elected mayor.[188]

One might think that as mayor of an important southern border city greatly affected by the consequences of illegal immigration, Faulconer would be sympathetic to Trump's policy agenda. Yet he definitely is not. Faulconer has criticized the Trump temporary travel ban,[189] given "unwavering support" to ties with Mexico,[190] issued a memorandum opposing Trump's immigration reforms,[191] denounced Trump's pullout from the Paris climate accord,[192] and joined the other Democrat mayors in the state in opposing the border wall just miles away from his City Hall.[193] He told the press he "would not be voting" for Donald Trump after Trump had clinched the Republican nomination.[194] As a Republican, he could have been a useful bridge for the Trump administration to other city officials in the state; however, he will not be much of a real player in California's growing conflict with Donald Trump. In late June 2017, Faulconer announced he would not be a candidate for governor in 2018.[195]

14. Almost Player: Eric Holder

Dubiously and separately, after Brown's appointment of Becerra as California attorney general, the California legislature "braced for a Trump presidency" by retaining President Obama's US Attorney General Eric Holder as an outside legal counsel.[196] "Having the former attorney general of the United States brings us a lot of firepower in order to prepare and safeguard the values of the people of California," Senate President Pro Tempore Kevin de León said in an interview. "This means we are very, very serious."[197] Holder was asked to provide specifics regarding how he plans to "assist" California Democrats—at a reported rate of some $25,000 per month—and his answer was, "Well."[198]

Holder made history of his own when in 2012 he became the first attorney general ever to be held in contempt of Congress for his failure to turn over documents related to the "Fast and Furious" scandal, which involved selling guns to Mexican drug cartels. The scandal erupted on the national stage when one of those guns was confirmed to have been used to kill a US border control agent, Brian Terry.[199]

The constitutionality of Holder's hire by legislators was immediately challenged by California State Assemblyman Kevin Kiley, R-Roseville.[200] In an inquiry letter to the state Attorney General's Office, Kiley cited a court ruling that said the state Constitution forbids hiring outside consultants for roles that can be carried out "adequately and competently" by those in the civil service, including work "defending California against federal actions."[201]

The legislature extended Holder's contract through the end of May, but no one really ever knew what Holder's role involved, or why the legislature paid Holder's firm Covington & Burling $25,000 per month out of the Assembly and Senate's operating budgets. On June 1, 2017, Senate President de León's office announced it would not renew Holder's contract but would continue to receive guidance from him.[202]

Kiley apparently continued his inquiries of the attorney general, all of which were ignored. An attorney and former deputy attorney general, Kiley explained his frustration with Attorney General Xavier Becerra's office in a Facebook post on May 24:[203]

We've learned a few things in the months since my initial request: (1) the constitutional issues relating to this Contract are apparently so complex that the Attorney General's Office, with its 1,592 attorneys and legal staff, needs more than four months to prepare an opinion; (2) most of the work Mr. Holder is doing remains a mystery, as requests for information have been rebuffed pursuant to "attorney-client privilege"; (3) despite the fact that the Legislature as a whole is Mr. Holder's client, he has refused to meet with any Republican legislators; (4) what is known of Mr. Holder's activities is duplicative of the activities of CA Attorney General Xavier Becerra, such as filing separate amicus briefs in a case relating to Sanctuary Cities; (5) a taxpayer-funded turf war between Mr. Becerra and Mr. Holder has developed, with Mr. Becerra opening his own office in Washington D.C. near Mr. Holder's office and publicly casting doubt on the need for Mr. Holder's services.

California's Economy: Taxed and Regulated

● ● ●

GOVERNOR JERRY BROWN AND HIS fellow liberal Democrats like to brag that California would have "the sixth-largest economy in the world" if it were its own country.[204] "It's a statement of the size and significance of the state's economy to the world, and the United States," said one university official.[205] PolitiFact California, a nonpartisan fact-checking organization, has said the claim, also made by State Attorney General Xavier Becerra on ABC News[206] and Senate President Pro Tempore Kevin de León in an address at the 2016 Democratic National Convention, is only "mostly true."[207] PolitiFact says the claim "ignore(s) California's sky high cost of living and Silicon Valley's role in the state's economic growth. The state's GDP drops several places when adjusted for cost of living."[208]

Cost of living is a big factor in California's economy, especially regarding housing costs. The state's great weather, coastline, mountains and natural beauty make housing in California more desirable and therefore more expensive than housing in other states. Yet, the high cost of living in the state is something that Democrat leaders like Brown, Becerra, and de León are not as well quoted on and really don't like to talk about. This is because for the last three years, the state has had the highest poverty rate in the nation when cost of living is taken into account,[209] according to the US Census Bureau.[210] California's top "real" poverty rate in the nation is well documented and has been acknowledged by PolitiFact, which backed up the claim made by Assembly Republican Leader Chad Mayes in January 2017 that California has "the highest poverty rate in the nation" when considering the US Census Bureau's Supplemental Poverty Measure.[211] Liberal Democrat policies have raised income, sales taxes, and consumption taxes on, for example, gasoline in the state to the highest levels in the nation. When these tax levies are calculated into the cost of living, they have clearly contributed to pushing California's cost of living higher and higher, hurting its poorest residents the most. When added to the high cost of housing, California's continually higher gasoline taxes, higher state and local sales taxes, and rising utility and electricity rates[212] to accommodate California's anti–fossil fuel "green policies" have their worst effect on California's poor, who can least afford the increases and are made poorer by them.

If California is indeed the sixth-largest economy in the world, something the state's liberal leaders want ownership of and look to with pride, these leaders can also be said to be presiding over an economy that would have the highest poverty rate in the world among the top six nations. That conclusion, especially to the extent that their tax and regulatory policies may contribute to increasing the state's already high cost of living and the financial burden on the poor, is surely nothing to brag about. Nevertheless, it is with this back-drop of a big economy, but with far too much poverty, that we consider how the Trump administration's economic policies and the work of California's Democrat leaders in the State Capitol, may jibe, or conflict, and may help or hurt Californians going forward.

President Trump's Vision for the Economy

The economic agenda President Trump campaigned on was explained in detail on August 6, 2016, in a speech to the Detroit Economic Club.[213] In his speech, Trump stated his goal of "providing the tools to every American to succeed economically" and to "unleash the American economy to spur faster growth." The vision he expressed was to increase productivity and entre-preneurship, "bringing prosperity, creating jobs and improving the lives of working families." He criticized Hillary Clinton's support for higher taxes and the "status quo" on economic policy, which had resulted in remarkably slow economic growth during the eight years of the Obama administration and a significant weakening of the economic power of the middle class.[214] The "four pillars" of economic reform Trump laid out in Detroit included tax reform, trade reform, regulatory reform, and energy reform.

On taxes, Trump outlined a plan to dramatically reduce them for individuals and businesses and present "the biggest tax reform since Reagan." Trump further promised to issue an executive order to impose "a regulatory moratorium on new agency regulations," "repeal and replace Obamacare," and initiate a targeted review "for regulations that inhibit hiring," specifically citing the Clean Power Plan of the Environmental Protection Agency (EPA), "which forces investment in renewable energy at the expense of coal and natural gas, raising electricity rates," and the Department of the Interior's moratorium on coal mining permits, "which put tens of thousands of coal miners out of work."

TRUMP WANTS LOWER TAXES
CALIFORNIA'S LEADERS KEEP RAISING TAXES

In highly taxed California, one would think the Trump policy on tax reform might be well received by the 58 percent of Californians who say they pay more taxes to state and local governments than they feel they should.[215] At 13.3 percent, California's top marginal income tax rate[216] seems drastic, especially when paired with the Obama administration's top marginal tax rate of 39.6 percent.[217] When combined, 52.9 percent is a lot of income tax to pay even for successful people. Trump has viewed addressing the persistent postrecession problems of slow economic growth, underemployment, and the middle class having a reduced share of the economy through the lens of reforming the federal tax system. He promised to significantly reduce high federal income tax rates to spur growth, including improving the international competitiveness of US businesses by reducing our nation's corporate tax rate, which is nearly the highest in the world.[218]

Nevertheless, after the 2016 general election, congressional Democrats huddled and decided that they would try to thwart Republican plans to overhaul the US tax code by portraying cuts as a "boon for the rich that betrays President-elect Donald Trump's campaign promise to fight for working Americans."[219] Yet those Democrats had not only lost the presidency, but they remained minorities in both Houses of Congress, yielding Trump and congressional Republicans great power.

California state government, however, saw a much different outcome at the polls in the same election. Democrats seized two-thirds majorities in both houses of the state legislature, putting them in a position to raise taxes by purely partisan voting. As a result of the 2014 elections, Democrats also controlled every single statewide constitutional office in the state. California's liberal Democrat leaders have an opposite view to Trump's advocacy of tax cuts. And history shows they are not alone in failing to see the value in reducing taxes to individuals, the middle class, and the business community. Having won an election spurred on by public outrage over increases in vehicle taxes, in 2008, even Republican Governor Arnold Schwarzenegger reversed course and proposed significant increases in taxes.[220] But it has been the liberal Democrats who have really built California's current onerous tax burden. Within two years of his election in 2010, Brown proposed and won at the ballot box the Proposition 30 tax hike, which "temporarily" raised state income taxes and sales taxes to the highest in the nation, generating $7 billion a year in new additional revenue for the state, through a tax increase that *Sacramento Bee* columnist Dan Walters later said "perhaps wasn't needed after all."[221] Brown won an extension of the "temporary" high state income tax until 2030 at the ballot box again in 2016, then successfully urged his colleagues in the state legislature to impose yet an additional $52 billion in new gas and vehicle taxes[222] in 2017, raising those taxes and fees to highest-in-the-nation levels, although with not a vote to spare.

Voter support for this cavalcade of taxation has started to erode, especially because of the gas tax increase. As taxpayers began to feel the effects of other taxes on their pocketbooks in June 2017, UC Berkeley's Institute of Governmental Studies found that 58 percent of Californians opposed the gas tax increase, with just 35 percent in favor, and a recall campaign was under way against a key Democrat state senator in a "swing" district who had provided the critical vote for passage of the tax increase.[223]

Whereas California's liberal Democrat leaders are good at raising taxes, they are not so good at reducing spending, at least in the opinion of the *Orange County Register*. Brown's proposed budget calls for a record $183.4 billion in state spending for the 2018 fiscal year, projecting a $400 million deficit, about which the *Register* wrote, "it is incredible that there is a deficit at all, given all the tax increases Californians and the Legislature have passed in recent years (and still more tax/fee increases and bond proposals on the horizon)."[224]

Thus, reducing taxes as a policy to improve the economy is surely not the view of California's liberal Democrat leaders, who tax, then tax yet again. "Californians already carry the nation's heaviest state income tax burden by far," writes George Skelton of the *Los Angeles Times*.[225] Skelton, who worries that California's tax system relies too heavily on taxing the rich, says that Californians will pay $83 billion in just state income taxes in 2017, with state sales, real property, and other taxes adding much more to the state's coffers.

Dan Walters for the *Sacramento Bee* adds, "we not only pay a lot of taxes that are obvious, such as those on income, retail sales and automotive fuel, but many that are virtually hidden,"[226] citing $2.3 billion in "vehicle license fees," which Walters says are really a property tax on cars and trucks based on their value. According to Walters, Californians pay $250 billion a year in taxes, with about $150 billion collected by the state and another $100 billion by local governments.

The huge amount of taxes California imposes and collects seems to put, for example, Trump's proposed national cut of the EPA's budget of 31 percent, or $2.6 billion, to a new budget of $5.65 billion into some perspective. Although Steve Lopez of the *Los Angeles Times* exaggerates the budget reduction proposal as a "dismantling" of EPA,[227] the budget cut by the Trump administration is literally a "drop in the bucket" in comparison not only to the $4.1 trillion Trump proposed in his first national budget, for a nation desperately in need of trimming $20 trillion in deficit, but also the hundreds of billions of dollars more collected annually by California state and local governments, much of which is focused on the environment.

A sad example of the disconnect on tax policy between President Trump and California's liberal leaders, and a coming area of conflict, is inheritance taxes. In his Detroit Economic Club speech, Trump singled out the high 40 percent federal "death tax" as an example of a tax he intended to repeal. Although that might be welcome news to owners of family farms and businesses in California, which the federal estate tax hits the hardest,[228] and who might appreciate the tax relief, under legislation introduced after the election by State Senator Scott Wiener, D-San Francisco, a ballot proposition will ask voters to approve keeping an identical estate tax in California after all, if Trump is successful in repealing the federal tax.[229] California does not have an estate tax, and the federal tax generated an estimated $4.5 billion in federal revenue from California in 2015.[230] If Wiener's proposition passes, California would initiate its own inheritance tax and gobble up that tax revenue, with really no expressed rationale for doing so other than spite against Trump's tax policies.

California's reflexive proclivity to increase taxes rather than reduce or reform them has a lot to do with long-term failures of policy makers to control spending, especially the public employee pension system in the state. And public employees are powerful political allies of the liberal Democrats who run things in Sacramento,[231] injecting millions into the political system to keep taxes high and elect liberal Democrats. The result has been inaction on reforming California's overly generous public employee pension system.

CALIFORNIA'S LOOMING PENSION-FUNDING CRISIS

In 2015, a study by Transparent California found that there were 625,000 people drawing pensions from the California Public Employees Retirement System and that 20,900 of those retired workers were making more than $100,000 a year in benefits.[232]

Governor Brown's 2017–2018 proposed state budget admits to $205.9 billion in "unfunded liabilities" for these pensions and health care for state employees.[233] Retirement liabilities, according to the budget document, have grown $51 billion in the last year alone "due to poor investment returns," among other explanations.[234] Payments by the state to the retirement fund are currently about $5.8 billion annually and "on track to nearly double" to $9.2 billion in six years.[235] These transfers are a significant part of the state budget, but many observers feel it is not enough.

A Stanford University study revealed that California's public employee pensions are underfunded by $1 trillion, or $93,000 per household in the state.[236] California's annual budget under Brown is therefore dwarfed by the pension obligations Stanford projects. George Mason University's Mercatus Center calculates California's unfunded pension liabilities at $757 billion and ranks

California's fiscal health at forty-fourth among the US states and Puerto Rico.[237] State tax revenues are said to exceed expenses by 4 percent, but the heavy reliance on debt and the whopping unfunded public employee pension liabilities drive California's financial solvency to nearly the bottom of all the states.

Rather than address this ominous problem, California's leaders have chosen to shift spending priorities and reduce public services in favor of protecting pensions and continually raising taxes, with little concern for reducing spending or reforming the pension system to reduce the high tax burden in the state.

TRUMP WANTS LESS REGULATION
CALIFORNIA'S LEADERS WANT EVEN MORE REGULATION

In his first week in office, President Trump issued an executive order intended to streamline and expedite environmental reviews and approvals for high-priority infrastructure projects.[238] An example of such a project is the TransCanada Keystone Pipeline for the importation of petroleum from Canada to the United States, a major economic project that had been mired in regulations and ultimately rejected during the Obama administration.[239] Trump, seeing the project as necessary for economic development, invited TransCanada to resubmit its application within days in office.[240] He cited the Obama administration's own environmental analysis that the Keystone Pipeline would support 42,100 jobs and create $2 billion in earnings within the United States in expressing the benefits of the project.[241]

Trump's campaign promises in his Detroit speech to reduce federal regulations on coal mining and use, for example, were not made without an understanding of the cost and benefits of such regulation. In signing an executive order to roll back the Obama administration's Clean Power Plan, the US Chamber of Commerce noted that the cost of Obama's planned regulations would be to "put 224,000 Americans out of work" annually and "cost $51 billion in gross domestic product loss,"[242] thus slowing economic growth and hurting the middle class emerging from the postrecession era.

The fundamental underpinning of Trump's philosophy—and, for that matter, Republican regulatory philosophy in general, especially during the

Reagan years—is the use of "cost–benefit" analysis in the promulgation of rules that affect the economy. When a regulation is considered and before it is adopted, not only are the benefits to society considered, but they are also balanced against the costs to society of the new rule. When the costs to society outweigh the benefits, the rule should be rejected.

CALIFORNIA'S "WAR ON CARBON"

Although the Trump approach appears rooted in cost-benefit analysis, in that it considers the costs of the regulations to society in terms of lost jobs and harm to the economy in balance with the alleged benefits, it seems to stand in stark contrast to California's Democrat leaders' idea of regulatory power, perhaps exemplified best by their own "War on Carbon" no matter the cost to society.

In what one news agency termed a "fiery" State of the State address[243] just after President Trump's inauguration, Governor Brown pushed back on expected new federal policies on immigration, health care, and climate change. "Whatever they do in Washington, they can't change the facts. And these are the facts: The climate is changing, the temperatures are rising and so are the oceans. Natural habitats everywhere are under increasing stress. The world knows this." But perhaps all the facts are not really that well understood by California's leaders.

News reports do persist that cities, like Los Angeles, continue to lead the nation in the ozone pollution[244] that scientists say contributes to climate change. Yet, more penetrating research suggests that federal and state anti-smog regulations have made great progress to date and have significantly reduced pollution in the state and particularly in the Los Angeles basin, perhaps calling into question the value to society of even further job-killing rules. Southern California's children have "significantly fewer respiratory symptoms as a result of improved air quality" over the last 20 years, according to what is termed the "landmark" USC Children's Health study.[245] The study found that particulate matter, which can penetrate deep into the lungs and cause serious health problems—dropped by 47 percent from 1992 to 2011.[246] Nitrogen dioxide decreased by 49 percent in the same two decades. USC researchers linked the drop in nitrogen dioxide with a 21 percent decrease in bronchial symptoms in children with asthma and a 16 percent decline of bronchial symptoms in those without asthma.[247] Whereas at one time California may have had the worst air quality in the world, Dr. Alan Lloyd, a former chair of the California Air Resources Board and former secretary of the California Environmental Protection Agency, states that despite growth, air quality in the state has improved "75–90% over the past 40 years."[248]

Other research shows that greenhouse-gas emissions in the state fell by 9 percent between 2004 and 2014, according to data compiled by the California Air Resources Board. Although more recent statistics aren't yet available, the air board itself says it believes emissions are continuing to fall.[249] It also concludes that the state is on track to meet its target of reducing annual emissions to 431 million metric tons by 2020, the same amount of greenhouse-gas pollution it produced in 1990, despite growth. "Emissions are going down," says an attorney with the Environmental Defense Fund, who adds the current clean-air rules are "working at what it set out to do."[250]

Regardless of the consistent and long-term progress on emission reduction, many Californians are fearful of politicians' continuing claims regarding the need for even more regulation, regardless of the cost to society, regarding climate change and carbon emission. The *San Diego Union-Tribune* reports that almost fifteen thousand "scientists and their supporters" gathered in San Diego to "champion science in decision making,"[251] with much of the reporting critical of the Trump administration's regulatory reforms, citing proposed budget cuts of 31 percent to the Environmental Protection Agency and 18 percent to the National Institutes of Health. This "politicization of science" is something that has been decried by organizations like the Cato Institute, which states that the "conflation of political agendas with science is destroying the credibility of academia."[252] It is also incomplete science, a "cherry-picking" of sciences, that elevates just biological science, even with the smallest of impacts, while failing to consider and balance for economic science and consideration of the full consequences of regulation to humanity.

Despite increasing reductions in environmental pollution as new, cleaner automobiles and trucks steadily replace older, dirtier ones in the state fleet, California's vehicle emission regulations are scheduled to become increasingly much stricter, especially from 2022–2025, through new rules the Obama administration "hastily approved before Trump took office."[253] "We are not backing down," said one member of the California Air Resources Board.

California has a rare power known as a "waiver" from federal standards that allows the state to impose its own emission rules for cars and trucks. As a result, the auto industry is forced to manufacture one set of vehicles complying with national rules and a different set complying with California's much stricter rules. This "waiver" is the basis for the establishment of Air Resources Board controls throughout the state. The waiver, or series of waivers, was granted decades ago when smog pollution was a much more pronounced problem in the state, especially in the Los Angeles basin. As we have seen, air pollution has already been steadily and significantly reduced in the state as a result of both federal and state regulations, and it will continue to decrease without further regulation over time as new, cleaner vehicles navigate the highways. But after President Obama was elected, liberal Democrat politicians in the state and in Washington, DC, expanded the waiver far beyond addressing air pollution to incorporate climate-change issues such as reduction of "greenhouse-gas emissions." The result has been a proliferation of new additional regulations in California not just to combat smog and air pollution but also to rapidly shift the state's very economy away from the use of fossil fuels.

The "centerpiece" of California's effort to address climate change is an auction system for pollution credit that is known as "cap and trade."[254] The idea is a permit system for controlling carbon emissions and other forms of atmospheric pollution by which an upper limit is set on the amount a given business or other organization may produce but that allows further capacity to be bought from other organizations that have not used their full allowance. However, the program is not going very well. The *Sacramento Bee* has written that the policy has faltered badly in the past year. Businesses have bought far fewer credits than expected, depriving the state of an expected windfall for such big-ticket items as high-speed rail.[255] The California Chamber of Commerce even filed a lawsuit against the program, arguing that it essentially amounts to an unconstitutional tax on businesses,[256] which would have required a two-thirds vote, consistent with the state constitution, in both houses of the state legislature to create. Instead, cap and trade was created through only a majority vote along partisan lines, with Democrats making the majority. The liberal California Supreme Court declined to consider an appeal from a lower court ruling against the Chamber of Commerce, thus upholding the program, and the program overcame hurdles in July 2017 when new legislation extended it well into the future.[257] California's climate-change efforts obviously come at a cost to Californians, both rich and poor.

In fact, a Stanford University energy economist has stated that California's policies on climate change are a "potential time bomb."[258] In Danny Cullenward's expert opinion, according to the *Los Angeles Times*, "[t]he state wants to slash greenhouse gas emissions so deeply in the coming years that oil refineries and other industries could face skyrocketing costs to comply with regulations, driving up gasoline prices until the system loses political support. If that happens, an effort touted as an international model for fighting global warming could collapse." Cullenward's observation that California's regulations are going too far is rooted in California's policy makers' failure to adequately consider not only the benefits but also the costs to society—especially to California's highest-in-the-nation poor population who depend upon affordable gas and utility bills—of climate-change rules. An area of a brewing controversy between the state and the Trump administration in future will be about the continuation of the waivers from federal standards, especially where there is federal disagreement of the cost/benefit to society of the California climate-change rules being proposed.

During his confirmation hearings, the new administrator of the Environmental Protection Agency (EPA), Scott Pruitt, said that he "cannot commit to keeping in place the current version of a decades-old federal waiver that allows California to set emissions standards stricter than elsewhere in the United States,"[259] although by June 2017, he told a congressional committee "[c]urrently the waiver is not under review."[260] A test of a potential conflict on the continued extension of the California waiver may be found in a lawsuit filed by industry on an EPA waiver decision in 2013 that allowed California to require additional emission filters on bulldozers, forklifts, and other diesel-powered equipment. The case is winding its way up the appellate court level, and Trump administration officials have told the court that now they are not sure if the specific 2013 waiver should have been granted at all.[261]

The conflict between California's liberal lawmakers and Trump's EPA was expanded to political grandstanding in April 2017 when State Attorney General Xavier Becerra filed a Freedom of Information Act request to compel the agency to turn over documents alleging that Pruitt, a former Oklahoma attorney general, has potential conflicts of interest with his past ties to the fossil-fuel industry.[262] The move by Becerra was said to be an attempt to force Pruitt to comply with federal ethics rules requiring Pruitt to disclose potential conflicts of interest, but the insinuation of federal ethics violations and the enforcement of such federal laws are far afield from the jurisdiction of the California attorney general.

CALIFORNIA'S PROLIFERATION OF RULEMAKING

California's almond and pistachio farmers occupy a major multibillion-dollar US agricultural role, providing heart-healthy nuts throughout the nation and the world. However, in recent years, prices have been hard-pressed, down as much as 50 percent in the wake of record harvests.[263] The EPA under the Trump administration, hailed by the California Farm Bureau, decided to halt Obama administration plans to prohibit the use of a popular and long-used pesticide by the farmers.[264] To the contrary, and with little consideration for the trials and tribulations of state agriculture producers, California environmentalists filed suit in the liberal US Ninth Circuit Court of Appeals to reinstate the ban planned by the Obama administration, a ban that would require the farmers to scramble for other, more expensive ways to protect crops against pests at the worst possible economic time for the industry.

Thus played out one of President Trump's first actions in office, which was to issue a "regulatory freeze" notice to all the heads of executive departments and agencies, consistent with his promise at the Detroit Economic Club speech.[265] The president followed this step with an executive order requiring agencies to identify at least two existing rules to be repealed upon the proposal of any new rule.[266]

There can be no starker contrast between the Trump administration's desire to reduce unnecessary regulations and California's efforts to expand them than the case of the Bay Area Air Quality Management District (BAAQMD). Even with the progress in reducing carbon, powerful government agencies in California like BAAQMD look for more and more regulation in their fields as the emphasis is expanded beyond addressing air pollution to impose rules justified by climate change, with not much expression of concern about the cost-benefit of the rules. BAAQMD[267] issues permits in nine counties and regulates air quality in the entire San Francisco Bay Area, and the agency is proposing a startlingly intrusive regional scheme that will promise "big changes in residents lives," according to the *San Francisco Chronicle*.[268] Its climate-change-justified plan includes the imposition of eighty-five new regulatory measures on businesses and individuals to attack "global warming" to further reduce emissions that have already been greatly reduced over the last twenty years. The climate-protection manager for the district, which covers nearly eight million people, was quoted as saying of the new program, which will include a campaign against meat production, "[t]hat doesn't mean everyone has to become vegan…[w]e just have to do everything we can, and probably changing our diets is part of that." Among the eighty-five proposed regulations are stricter emission rules for refineries, dairies, landfills, and water treatment plants; slower driving and tougher carpool rules; and "making roads friendlier for electric cars,"[269] along with higher freeway tolls, less on-street parking, higher gasoline taxes, and restrictions on home water heaters and heating systems fueled by gas, among many other ideas, many of which might strike non-Californians and some Californians alike as excessive.

In fact, as to dairies, California's liberal officials across the state have been particularly concerned about promulgating new regulations on "bovine entric fermentation," commonly referred to as "cow farts." In September 2016, Governor Brown signed a bill against the wishes of the state's dairy farmers to curb "these dangerous pollutants" to "slow climate change."[270] The legislation allows for the Air Resources Board to regulate cow flatulence and pursue technologies to do so. The significant increase in composting required by the law will surely raise the cost of milk for all Californians, but it will especially hit the state's poorest residents, who rely more on milk protein for their families' nutrition.

Californians do have a much different view on environmental regulation than the rest of the country. According to the Public Policy Institute of California, 56 percent of state residents say regulations are necessary to protect the public interest, and 54 percent say stricter environmental laws and regulations are worth the costs.[271] A historic milestone in the state that is conceded to have affected voters' attitudes for the last generations is the 1969 Santa Barbara oil spill. That spill spread three million gallons of gooey tar on thirty-five miles of pristine beaches between Ventura and Santa Barbara counties, a heavily Republican area at that time, killing thousands of fish, birds, and sea mammals and fostering California's significant conservation and antipollution effects from that point forward,[272] including attitudes about climate change today. Today, 81 percent of Californians believe that global warming is a serious issue.[273] Yet, according to a Pew Research national poll, only 36 percent of Americans are personally very concerned about climate change as an issue, 38 percent have just "some" concern about it, and 26 percent are not really concerned about it at all.[274] Divisions on the issue are highly polarized by political party.[275] Trust in climate-change scientists is particularly low among Republicans nationwide, most of whom do not agree that climate scientists should have a major role in policy decisions.[276] These divergences in polling results offer a useful insight into the differences in attitudes Californians have on environmental regulation in contrast to the rest of the nation, and they help explain why California is so out of step with the rest of the nation politically.

The "Clean Power Plan" and Paris Climate Agreement

Trump's Detroit speech offered strong opposition to the Obama administration's Clean Power Plan, which comprised aggressive attempts to reduce carbon emissions, and keeping his campaign promise, after the election Trump signed an executive order to undo the plan.[277] According to the US Chamber of Commerce, Obama's carbon regulations could "put 224,000 Americans out of work" annually, "cost $51 billion on Gross National Product loss," and "lower disposable household income by $586 billion."[278] The Clean Power Plan was considered the central part[279] of President Obama's commitment to the Paris climate agreement.

Trump also opposed the Paris Agreement during his campaign, and he has said that he would like to see the United States withdraw from it.[280] The Clean Power Plan of the Obama administration was a part of the comprehensive "national climate plans" that countries submitted to participate in the Paris climate agreement.

Predictably, Governor Brown loves the Paris climate agreement. The California governor even attended the December 2015 United Nations summit on climate change in Paris as a representative of a "nonparty stakeholder" while the agreement was being finalized. As the *Los Angeles Times* reported, "[t]he governor has pushed for slashing oil consumption and boosting renewable energy in California. But he went further in his comments in Paris, calling for nothing less than a radical transformation of life on Earth. 'Instead of being a burden, it's really an opportunity to live lighter on the planet,' he said during one event. 'Friendship, beauty, art has to take the place of this heavy commodification of our entire existence.'"[281]

In the Paris Agreement, world governments agreed to the long-term goal of keeping the increase in global temperature to two degrees centigrade above "preindustrial" levels; to attempt to lower global temperature by more; to peak global carbon emissions as soon as possible, "recognizing that this will take longer for developing countries"; and to undertake rapid reductions thereafter in accordance with the best available science.[282] President Obama pledged that the United States would strive to reduce greenhouse-gas emissions by a target of as much as 28 percent below 2005 levels by 2025.[283] He also pledged $3 billion to help developing foreign countries reduce their emissions.

Although the accord is very strongly supported by climate-change advocates around the world, there is doubt the Paris Agreement really does much to actually help mitigate global warming. As environmental researcher Bjorn Lomborg has written, even if all the Paris parties fulfill every promise contained in their submissions by 2030, the total temperature reduction will be 0.048°C (0.086°F) by 2100.[284] That change is less than the current margin of error estimates of .08°C for annual average global temperature. The reduction in the next twenty-five years will be even smaller—too small to affect weather patterns, polar animal populations, or any significant climatic factor.

The United States is not the world's biggest emitter of carbon. Rather, China is the top polluter in the world.[285] Carbon dioxide emissions from China account for 30 percent of global greenhouse-gas emissions; the United States, at 15 percent, is at just half of what China emits.[286] Although direct comparison of the commitments China and the United States made in the Paris Agreement is tricky because of opaque comparative terminologies and nonbinding aspects in the agreement on carbon, "Carbon Tracker" has indicated that China's target for 2020 under the Paris Agreement is a 20 percent[287] reduction in its emissions,[288] which is numerically a significantly lighter burden on the world's biggest greenhouse-gas emitter than the 28 percent burden the Obama administration negotiated.[289]

China doesn't just pollute in its own country. Although China's use of coal (considered one of the single biggest contributors to climate change) has begun to decrease in the last few years, and despite the Paris Agreement, it continues to be the world's largest exporter of coal-related financing and equipment, and its state-owned companies are involved in a hundred coal-fired power projects around the globe, in nations that rank among the most vulnerable to the damaging effects of climate change (according to climate-change advocates), including Pakistan, India, Indonesia, Vietnam, Mongolia, and Iran.[290]

The Competitive Enterprise Institute (CEI), a Washington, DC–based think tank, has determined that the United States "cannot comply with the Paris Agreement and pursue a pro-growth energy agenda. Affordable, plentiful, reliable energy is the lifeblood of modern economic life. Yet, the Paris Agreement's central goal is to make fossil fuels, America's most plentiful and affordable energy source, more expensive across the board."[291] Urging President Trump to end America's participation in the Paris Agreement, CEI states that the agreement "will produce no detectable climate benefits" and will instead "divert trillions of dollars from productive investments that would advance global welfare to political uses."[292]

So, on June 1, in a White House Rose Garden ceremony, President Trump fulfilled his campaign pledge and announced that the United States would cease all implementation of the agreement. In justifying his action, Trump said, "[t]he Paris Climate Accord is simply the latest example of Washington entering into an agreement that disadvantages the United States to the exclusive benefit of other countries, leaving American workers—who I love—and taxpayers to absorb the cost in terms of lost jobs, lower wages, shuttered factories, and vastly diminished economic production." In support, he offered statistics:

Compliance with the terms of the Paris Accord and the onerous energy restrictions it has placed on the United States could cost America as much as 2.7 million lost jobs by 2025 according to the National Economic Research Associates. This includes 440,000 fewer manufacturing jobs—not what we need—believe me, this is not what we need—including automobile jobs, and the further decimation of vital American industries on which countless communities rely. They rely for so much, and we would be giving them so little. According to this same study, by 2040, compliance with the commitments put into place by the previous administration would cut production for the following sectors: paper down 12 percent; cement down 23 percent; iron and steel down 38 percent; coal—and I happen to love the coal miners—down 86 percent; natural gas down 31 percent. The cost to the economy at this time would be close to $3 trillion in lost GDP and 6.5 million industrial jobs, while households would have $7,000 less income and, in many cases, much worse than that.[293]

Yet even as America withdraws from the Paris Agreement, California officials say they will not! Brown has called for a "countermovement" for what he feels would be "a colossal mistake" to leave the agreement.[294] He even told a group of climate scientists at a conference in San Francisco that "California will take over leadership" on climate change if the United States pulls out of the agreement, with the suggestion being that California might try to join the accord on its own; regarding the constitutionality of this possibility, a Stanford Law school official said, "[t]he short answer is no."[295] On the eve of Trump's final decision to pull out of the agreement, Brown called on state governments to forge an alliance to support the Paris climate deal, even if the United States withdrew from it,[296] and subsequently Brown followed through by signing his own "nonbinding" agreement with China's Ministry of Science and Technology to collaborate on reducing greenhouse-gas emissions, telling the Associated Press that Trump's decision "will ultimately prove only a temporary setback."[297]

Trump Wants More, Cheaper Energy
California Wants Less, More Costly Energy

In a rare positive headline for the Trump administration, the *San Francisco Chronicle* wrote, "[f]or struggling Kern County, Trump means hope and change."[298] Home to Bakersfield, the state's ninth-largest city, Kern County delivered 53 percent of its votes to Donald Trump while most of the rest of the state was piling up votes for Hillary Clinton. Oil is an important business in Kern County, but in the past few years, eight thousand oil wells have been closed, putting thousands out of work.[299] Agriculture in the county has been hit as well, as a result of the water-access and government regulatory issues. The owner of one local business that services oil-field facilities said of Trump that he "has rough edges, there's no doubt about that. But you see what he's doing—cutting back on the EPA, building pipelines, and you like that."[300]

Trump indeed has kept his promise to reform energy policy. And Trump's reforms put him in conflict with resistant liberal California policy makers. Shortly after President Trump signed an executive order within the first one hundred days of his presidency to allow for the expansion of offshore oil drilling in federal waters, a liberal Democrat state senator from Santa Barbara announced state legislation to prevent new leases in state waters for construction of the new pipelines needed for expansion of the enormous industry of oil and gas development off the coast of California.[301]

Is there good news for California in a Trump economy?

Since Trump assumed office, national unemployment has decreased to the lowest level in sixteen years, especially for younger people and Hispanics.[302] Average hourly earnings for all employees have increased, and in the early months of the new administration, the nation gained over one hundred thousand construction and manufacturing jobs, a number that continues to grow every month.[303] Consumer confidence has also risen, as has positive business sentiment for the future.[304] Gallup's US Economic Confidence Index hit its highest weekly average in nine years during March 2017, showing that Americans are gaining economic optimism about the future.[305] Millions of Americans who have 401(k) pension plans invested in the stock market greatly benefitted from gains in the first one hundred days of Trump's presidency, where the market performed "well above average" under a Republican president, making a 5 percent gain in the S&P 500, according the business cable network CNBC.[306] Such economic gains are continuing.

The next recession "now appears further away thanks to Trump," according to Deutsche Bank's chief international economist.[307] A key plank in Trump's platform was improving the gross national product (GDP). Growing GDP means more tax revenue, even at lower rates, and more jobs and more wealth creation across the nation. Even before passage of his tax reform plan, the Trump administration is delivering on its promises to improve economic growth. In the first quarter of 2017, GDP grew 1.4 percent, according to the Commerce Department,[308] compared with –5.4 percent in the first quarter of the Obama administration.[309] In the second quarter of 2017, covering April through the end of June, pickups in consumer and business spending bumped GDP up 2.6 percent,[310] underscoring resilience in the economy and achieving in one quarter a growth level far above the Obama administration's performance for the entire eight years of that administration.

Californians, many of whom also have 401(k) pension plans and stock-market investments, should reap the rewards of an improved economy under President Trump. Yet others may not fare so well. Although construction jobs are growing nationally, by March 2017, they were still down in California by 17 percent compared with peak levels in February 2006.[311] As we have seen, the advantages to income earners of federal tax reduction under Trump are countered by the reality of California's punishingly high state and local taxes. Should the administration's tax reform include passage of a provision to eliminate the federal deduction for state income taxes, Californians, who pay high taxes to begin with, would be penalized even more on their federal tax filings.[312] And to the extent that the new administration is successful in reducing job-killing regulations, California will still have a strong regulatory framework intact to make business expansion more difficult in the state than it is in other states. Coupled with the unaddressed public employee pension crisis, and because of antibusiness state government policies, California under Trump will likely remain the least business-friendly state in the nation,[313] and that means continuing loss of opportunities for lifting the state's poorest residents out of poverty.

CNBC has commented that there are several ways the important technology industries in California and Silicon Valley may thrive under a Trump administration—namely, industry-specific regulation will likely diminish, the employee stock options that are commonly used in the technology industry will be a more useful incentive to induce new job candidates or keep tenured employees, labor rules will be more flexible, and corporate taxes will go down, thus improving profits.[314] Yet San Francisco is reported to be the top source of new workers moving to Seattle, followed by New York City and Chicago, as "Silicon Valley techies are fleeing" now.[315] California's high personal income taxes compared with those in Washington state, which doesn't even impose a state income tax,[316] may have something to do with the exodus.

There is other good economic news for Californians in Trump's presidency. Agriculture will benefit from reduced federal regulation of the environment, thus improving profits, creating jobs, and driving down the cost of food. Water issues may be resolved in favor of farmers as well, especially in connection with the one hundred million acres of land in California controlled by the federal government and as a result of the farm-friendly leadership in the Interior Department.[317] During his confirmation hearings, EPA Administrator Pruitt pointed out with disdain a $2.8 million fine that a Tehama County farmer was levied for plowing a field for a wheat crop on his own land, allegedly harming "wetlands."[318] Pruitt described the fine as an example of the government wrongly punishing farmers for doing their jobs.

There will also be a windfall from the proposed $54 billion hike in military spending and even from new funding for infrastructure, such as deferred maintenance for Yosemite and other national parks.[319] "The increase in defense spending will be disproportionately directed to California, as sophisticated airplanes, weaponry, missiles and ships require the technology that is produced here," wrote Jerry Nickelsburg, a UCLA senior economist. "Moreover, there are few places to build the proposed 150 new warships and San Diego is one of them. Regionally we expect a positive impact in the Bay Area and in coastal Southern California."[320]

In sum, Californians and the overall state economy will likely benefit from the policies of the Trump presidency. But these gains will surely be blunted by the continuing tax-spend-regulate policies of Brown and the liberal Democrats in control of state government, and the biggest losers, sadly, may be California's poorest residents.

Sanctuary Cities in a Sanctuary State

● ● ●

THERE IS PERHAPS NO MORE of a confrontational issue today between Washington, DC, and California as that of "sanctuary cities."

Among his first acts as president, Donald Trump issued Executive Order 13768 purporting to defund government entities that will not cooperate with federal immigration officials. House Republicans, with some bipartisan appeal, including twenty-four Democrat members of Congress, passed legislation in June 2017 known as "Kate's Law," which would impose tougher penalties on criminals entering the United States illegally multiple times, such as the criminal illegal alien who had been shielded from federal officials by San Francisco's sanctuary-city law and subsequently murdered Kate Steinle.[321] The House also passed a companion bill that would cut off some federal grants to sanctuary jurisdictions that limit cooperation with federal authorities.[322]

Yet at the same time, in California, the policy direction went the completely opposite direction. A federal judge in San Francisco blocked Trump's order on a lawsuit brought by the City of San Francisco, on the technicality that the government had not defined "sanctuary city" clearly enough,[323] and State Attorney General Xavier Becerra lead a group of ten state attorney generals, all from states that voted for Hillary Clinton in the presidential election, to file briefs in opposition to the administration in the case.[324]

The California State Senate has adopted legislation to expand sanctuary status and to make the entire state a "sanctuary state." In privileged Malibu, at the inspiration of liberal resident and actor Martin Sheen, the city council voted 3-2[325] to add its name to the growing list of forty or so sanctuary cities in the state.

Los Angeles Mayor Eric Garcetti said he will "fight efforts by the Trump administration to take away federal funding needed for law enforcement in Los Angeles," adding "[s]lashing funds for first-responders, for our port and airport, for counterterrorism, crime-fighting and community-building serves no one—not this city, not the federal government, not the American people."[326] Garcetti signed off on an executive order of his own barring law enforcement who patrol the city's port and airport from inquiring about a criminal suspect's immigration status.[327]

Garcetti's police chief said, "it's not our job" to help enforce federal immigration laws.[328] The Los Angeles Police Department has long abided by "Standard Order 40," which prohibits inquiring about a person's immigration status during a law-enforcement action or arresting someone specifically for violating immigration laws.[329]

"Standard Order 40" would appear to violate federal law requiring cooperation. Actually, standard police manuals in many other cities in California do, in fact, offer guidance on how to stop people suspected of illegally entering the United States, a misdemeanor under federal law.[330] In any event, Garcetti thus staked out what appears to be a contradictory position on Los Angeles's sanctuary laws: "we want federal money for law enforcement, but we won't do the work to enforce the law."

Republican mayor of San Diego Kevin Faulconer joined Garcetti in opposition to Trump's executive order by declaring that his city would not participate in any attempt to deputize local law-enforcement officers as Immigration and Customs Enforcement agents for the purpose of apprehending criminal illegal aliens.[331]

Similarly, in late March 2017, San Diego County was placed on a list by the Department of Justice as a jurisdiction that was failing to comply with routine detainer requests by the federal government to turn criminal illegal aliens in county jails over to ICE agents for processing. A complicating factor for many counties to honor such requests is another state law, known as the "Trust Act," which bars policing agencies from accepting criminal detainer requests from ICE in many cases.[332] The Trust Act also appears to violate federal law.

Despite the possibility of defunding, a Santa Ana city councilman said "[w]e will fight this vigorously and still continue to maintain services…[w]e are going to look into every single legal action we can to protect ourselves from the Department of Justice's plan."[333] San Francisco Mayor Ed Lee, whose city had sued to block the sanctuary-cities executive order, said the city would resist Trump's immigration policy and that "[s]trong cities like San Francisco must continue to push our nation forward, and let this once again be a reminder to America that we are a city that fights for what is right."[334] Mayors representing other declared sanctuary cities, including Berkeley, San Jose, and Oakland, have reportedly "thumbed their noses" at threats of federal funding cuts and insist they will work together "regionally" to offset any defunding from the federal government.[335] Are these mayors signaling yet additional new taxes on already heavily tax-burdened Californians to make up any difference in loss of federal funding to support their scofflaw sanctuary-city statuses? And one wonders where these mayors' anger was when the Obama administration, under US Attorney General Loretta Lynch, notified the state in July 2016 that funding under the criminal alien assistance program and other Department of Justice programs would be terminated if the state did not become compliant with federal immigration law, given that the Department's Inspector General had found California to be in violation of the law, with $135 million in federal grants at risk to help cover the cost of incarcerating criminal illegal aliens.[336] State Senate President Pro Tempore Kevin de León termed Trump administration follow-up on the jurisdictions identified by the Obama administration as violating federal law as "law enforcement policies on principles of white supremacy."[337]

Trump's executive order to defund sanctuary jurisdictions was not conjured up out of nowhere. Preexisting federal law at 8 *United States Code* Section 1373(a) requires local jurisdictions to cooperate with federal immigration authorities. It reads as follows:

> Notwithstanding any other provision of Federal, State, or local law, a Federal, State, or local government entity or official may not prohibit, or in any way restrict, any government entity or official from sending to, or receiving from, the Immigration and Naturalization Service information regarding the citizenship or immigration status, lawful or unlawful, of any individual.[338]

In a memorandum explaining Trump's order and offering a definition of "sanctuary" status, US Attorney General Jeff Sessions stated the determination of the administration that grants affected by the order would only be those administered by the Department of Justice and the Department of Homeland Security, and thus all federal funding for a sanctuary jurisdiction would not be at risk.[339] Some observers termed the Sessions memo as a "narrowing" of the definition of "sanctuary city" that limited potential financial consequences for noncompliant state and local governments.[340] Similarly, the House passed the No Sanctuary for Criminals Act, H.R. 3003, which will remove from eligibility for Department of Justice, Department of Homeland Security, and Immigration and Naturalization Service grants related to law enforcement, terrorism, national security, immigration, or naturalization for states and other jurisdictions that do not comply with the federal law requiring cooperation among federal and state and local agencies in executing federal immigration laws.[341]

CALIFORNIA SENATE BILL 54

The *Washington Post* noted, "[f]lipping a giant middle finger to President Trump, California is on its way to becoming the first sanctuary state in the nation."[342] "If Jeb Bush or Chris Christie or John Kasich had been elected, this bill would not be necessary," de León said. "These are extraordinary times."[343]

In early April 2017, in a strictly party-line vote, the California State Senate passed Senate Bill (SB) 54, introduced by President Pro Tempore Kevin de León.[344] "We are trying to make our communities safer and be intelligent about this," said de León, adding what would become a falsity, "no rhetoric and no bluster." However, the legislation was hardly uncontroversial, is full of rhetoric, and was heavily opposed by law enforcement. The bill bars local and state law enforcement from using their resources to help federal immigration enforcement.

Local law enforcement officials and some county sheriffs denounced the legislation, saying it could hinder their participation in task forces involving federal immigration agencies, and in the face of the opposition, de León allowed a few minor amendments to the bill.[345] The state must inform federal officials at least sixty days in advance of the release of illegal aliens with a prior *conviction* of a violent or serious felony. Of course, this means that illegals *charged* with such offenses would not be included in the notice, nor would they be if they have charges or convictions of violent or serious misdemeanors. For example, a prior conviction for possession of a stolen gun worth less $950 is a misdemeanor in California because of a change in the law known as "Proposition 47." Such a criminal would be concealed by the state from federal immigration enforcement under SB 54. "This bill is unsafe...is unlawful. This bill is designed to make California a sanctuary for certain dangerous criminals," said State Senator Jeff Stone, R-Temecula, who added that the bill might lose funding from the federal government if it is passed and signed into law.[346]

In arguing against the legislation to make California a sanctuary state, State Senator Joel Anderson, R-San Diego, said that without cooperation from local law enforcement agencies, federal officials would be forced into schools and neighborhoods to find illegal criminal aliens, potentially putting innocents at risk.[347]

Yet it was something of a surprise when California Supreme Court Chief Justice Tani G. Cantil-Sakauye wrote an open letter on March 16, 2017, to US Attorney General Jeff Sessions and Secretary of Homeland Security John Kelly complaining that US ICE agents were now using California courthouses as "bait" for arrests and a place for "stalking" immigrants who "pose no risk to public safety"[348] and demanded that ICE stop such arrest procedures. An ICE spokesperson responded that "[t]hese individuals, who often have significant criminal histories, are released onto the street, presenting a potential public safety threat," adding that when ICE Fugitive Operations officers go into a community to proactively locate criminal aliens, innocent bystanders can be put in harm's way, and that because of screening at courthouses, "safety risks for the arresting officers and for the arrestee are substantially diminished."[349]

Sessions and Kelly quickly wrote back in a letter dated March 29, 2017, that the chief justice's characterizations were "particularly troubling." They cited case law supporting that arrest of persons in a public place based on probable cause has long been held constitutionally permissible, and that ICE agents do not act indiscriminately and only seek the arrest of those who have been investigated and targeted, and they reminded Cantil-Sakauye that the word "stalking" has a specific separate legal meaning that is unrelated to the work of ICE officers. Of the problem of cooperation in California, they wrote:

> Some jurisdictions, including the state of California and many of its largest counties and cities, have enacted statutes and ordinances designed to specifically prohibit or hinder ICE from enforcing immigration law by prohibiting communication with ICE, and denying requests by ICE officers and agents to enter prisons and jails to make arrests. Such policies threaten public safety rather than enhance it. As a result, ICE officers and agents are required to locate and arrest these aliens in public places, rather than in secure jail facilities where the risk of injury to the public, the alien, and the officer is significantly increased because the alien can more readily access a weapon, resist arrest, or flee. Because courthouse visitors are typically screened upon entry to search for weapons and other contraband, the safety risks for the arresting officers and persons being arrested are substantially decreased.[350]

Sessions and Kelly told the chief justice that she should consider taking her concerns to the governor as well as cities and counties that limit local law enforcement's involvement with federal agents, rather than complaining to them about state policies that "occasionally necessitate ICE officers and agents to make arrests at courthouses and other public places."[351]

Critics warn that California's effusive sanctuary policies could undermine the state's ability to provide other services, in the threat of losing federal funding. A Hoover Institution research fellow told Politico that California's sanctuary strategy is akin to "waving a red flag in front of a bull." He continued, "The main thing it will accomplish is making Trump's policies on sanctuary cities more popular than they might be, while boxing in California legally... [i]f their position on California is that they will stand in the schoolhouse door and defy federal law, it's not going to play well for them."[352]

Californians Oppose Sanctuary Laws, Especially When Funding Is at Risk

Although California's liberal politicians in control of the state and many localities have rushed to enact and extend "sanctuary" laws, it would be incorrect to reflexively assume that Californians themselves are fully supportive of these efforts. In fact, as discerned by three different measures, Californians appear to oppose sanctuary laws.

In late 2015, before the presidential election, the UC Berkeley Institute of Governmental Studies conducted a scientific online survey of nearly 1,100 Californians and surprisingly found that 74 percent of respondents said that local authorities should not be able to ignore a federal request to hold a detained person who is in the country illegally. The poll found that almost two-thirds of Latinos shared this view in opposition to sanctuary cities. "We found very broad-based opposition to the idea of sanctuary cities," said the institute's director.[353]

The subsequent election, of course, brought sanctuary policies to the forefront of the policy debate, as it was highly associated with Trump's campaign issues, and Trump was a controversial candidate, especially in California. In March 2017, UC Berkeley polled registered voters again on the issue, and a majority of Californians, this time 53 percent, once again stated that they opposed the idea of cities and counties being allowed to ignore requests from federal authorities to detain illegal aliens who have been arrested and are about to be released.[354]

UC Berkeley found, however, that when the question was framed differently, and voters were asked if they supported or opposed sanctuary cities that instruct police to *automatically* turn illegal aliens over to federal authorities for possible deportation, the results became conflicted, and support for sanctuary cities improved to 56 percent, with 44 percent in opposition.

Importantly, however, about 20 percent of those favoring sanctuary cities in California say they are less inclined to support them if they put federal funding at risk.[355] When federal funding is at risk, there is credible evidence in the polling to conclude that a majority of Californians oppose sanctuary laws, even if police are required to *automatically* turn illegal aliens over to federal authorities.

It is revealing about the scope of the opposition to sanctuary laws to note that with California Republican Party registration statewide at an all-time low of 27.3 percent[356] this opposition to sanctuary laws crosses party lines quite significantly and greatly exceeds Trump's 31.5 percent vote share for president in the 2016 California general election.[357] The upshot is that there are plenty of Democrats and nonpartisan voters who united to join Republicans in responding to a poll that they opposed sanctuary laws in the state.

Largely because of law-enforcement opposition, even if SB 54 is signed into law by the governor, and California becomes a sanctuary state, some important local jurisdictions are likely to stage their own "resistance." For example, in El Dorado County, right next to Sacramento, Trump won the presidential election by 52.6 percent, with 38.9 percent for Hillary Clinton.[358] El Dorado Sheriff John D'Agostini, who runs a county jail that would have to limit cooperation with ICE under the state law, reportedly believes SB 54 is "tantamount to coddling criminals," and he will refuse to go along.[359] "I'm going to follow federal law on this issue," said D'Agostini on his actions if SB 54 is enacted. "It's concerning because it's going to put me crosswise with state law."[360] The county's district attorney added, "[t]here is no doubt we have a number of people in this county illegally who committed crimes…and those are the people SB 54 seeks to protect."[361]

In Fresno County, Sheriff Margaret Mims has been termed "a leader" in cooperating with ICE agents, where between June 2015 and February 2017, ICE took 322 people into custody from the Fresno jail, including a person who had been deported nineteen times.[362] According to Assemblyman Jim Patterson, R-Fresno, such cooperation "would cease to exist" under SB 54.[363]

Not only some sheriffs but even some mayors in California oppose sanctuary-city laws. Mayors of the cities of Escondido, Poway, and San Marcos, all near the border in San Diego County, joined at a press conference in opposition to SB 54. Also in attendance was El Cajon Mayor Bill Wells, who said that the proposed law would allow for more violent felons who otherwise could be deported to come back onto the streets. Wells added that the bill was more about political showmanship than protecting innocent immigrants. "We don't have the luxury of being able to make political points," he said, "[w]e have a job, an obligation, to keep all the people that live in our cities safe."[364]

Even the board of directors of the Bay Area Rapid Transit District "tapped the brakes" on a call to declare the transit system a "sanctuary" when federal funding was cited as being at risk. The BART General Counsel said the largely symbolic act "could be seen as provocative."[365]

IN SUM ON CALIFORNIA SANCTUARY STATUS

California is already riddled with existing rules and regulations that do not comply with federal statutes requiring cooperation on immigration enforcement, such as the Trust Act and the LAPD's long-standing "Standard Order 40." Recent declarations by various cities make the law even more in contempt of federal law, and SB 54 will simply add yet another layer of complications to efforts of the federal government, in both the Obama and the Trump administrations, to bring California into legal compliance. The issue is going to continue to fester until the Trump administration resolves court cases and actually establishes its authority to withdraw grant funding to the state, limited as it will be to grants from the Department of Justice and the Department of Homeland Security. At that point, the state and jurisdictions can decide if they are going to change their ways, or just attempt to further raise taxes on Californians to cover the added financial burden they will have created. The losers in this melodrama are the people of California, whose security is surely, in the end, put at risk by the politicians in the state.

Infrastructure Woes

● ● ●

ONLY A FEW WEEKS AFTER a defiant State of the State address by Governor Jerry Brown, citing "deep divisions across America" with the election of President Trump,[366] Northern California's big Oroville Dam, at full capacity due to a bountiful winter rainy season, began spilling over its emergency auxiliary spillway, causing local authorities to evacuate nearly two hundred thousand residents of the surrounding area.[367] Shortly thereafter, authorities warned that the emergency spillway was in danger of failing and could unleash uncontrolled floodwaters on the thousands of family homes in the towns below the dam.

The *San Jose Mercury News* reported that the spillway breakage was likely due to the refusal of the California State Department of Water Resources and the State Water Contractors, a group of twenty-seven water agencies, to make necessary repairs and structural improvements because they didn't want to be saddled with the cost.[368] Immediately following the flooding threat, Brown announced that he wanted to work with the new president on infrastructure projects.[369]

Trump, of course, made improving the nation's infrastructure one of the centerpieces of his campaign. On becoming president, he announced plans to support a $1 trillion bill to upgrade US bridges, roads, airports, and other public works.[370] His plans also include cutting red tape, such as overly burdensome environmental reviews that can slow down approvals; fostering public–private partnerships; attacking a broad range of projects, such as boosting broadband and rehabilitating veterans' hospitals; and focusing on shovel-ready projects.[371] On "shovel-ready," Trump said "[w]hen we do the infrastructure, it's going to be very important to me that if we give billions to a state, like New York, California, or any other state, that they're going to have to start spending the money, they're going to have approval within 120 days."[372]

Brown was right to try to open a door to Trump and surely needs to work with the administration on infrastructure to benefit California. He soon came up with a "$100 billion wish list" for federal assistance on infrastructure projects and repairs.[373]

Whether it is crumbling dams, shaky bridges, weak tunnels, pothole-filled highways and roads, regulatory shutdowns, or delays for the environment or near-extinct baitfish, California's infrastructure is a mess, and part of the mess is because liberal politicians like Brown have long made public employee union contracts, pensions, pandering to environmentalists, and increasing education spending at the behest of the California Teachers Association a higher priority than infrastructure.

When the money runs out from spending on their more favored priorities, or work is delayed because environmentalists complain about the impact on the environment of a public-works-project repair, the result is that a dam breaks, threatening hundreds of thousands, roads crumble, and public safety is diminished. Rather than adjusting priorities, the liberals in control either ignore the problem or just levy more taxes on Californians to claim they will fix what they should have been taking care of in the first place.

Even the *Los Angeles Times* acknowledged the state's infrastructure woes, writing in an editorial:

California has consistently failed to spend the money needed to keep the state's transportation infrastructure in good condition. Caltrans has deferred $59 billion worth of highway and bridge repairs. Cities and counties face an even bigger bill, needing $78 billion to return local streets to good condition. The state currently spends about $1.2 billion a year on highways and bridges, but it should be spending $800 million more each year just to stay current on the maintenance.[374]

California's infrastructure needs, according to the *Times*, far exceed what its liberal leaders are willing to pay.

In early April 2017, Senate Bill 1 was approved by both houses of the state legislature without a vote to spare in the state senate, increasing taxes by $52 billion over ten years[375] and raising the state's gas tax to the highest in the nation, under a promise that the money would be spent on infrastructure for roads and transportation. Critics are skeptical and say the state has squandered transportation funds in the past and spent the money elsewhere.[376] The tax is deeply unpopular, with 58 percent of voters opposing it and only 35 percent supporting it, according to a UC Berkeley Institute of Governmental Studies poll.[377]

While Brown and legislative Democrats prioritized and championed increased taxes, sanctuary for illegal aliens, admittance of more refugees, state payments for prison inmate sex-change operations, failed attempts to address homelessness, transgender bathrooms, climate-change awareness, and the hiring of Eric Holder to undermine the Trump administration, the Oroville Dam was crumbling. And they knew it. The *San Jose Mercury News* reported that state agencies ignored serious warnings about the dam first brought to their attention twelve years ago because, again, they did not want to incur the extra costs.[378]

In natural-disaster-prone California, with its earthquakes, mudslides, and forest fires, it is fair to ask, what tragedy will it take for the people of the state to hold elected politicians and government officials accountable?

What About Jerry Brown's Infrastructure Legacy?

"The cracks in the 50-year-old Oroville Dam, and the massive spillage and massive evacuations that followed, shed light on the true legacy of Jerry Brown," demographer Joel Kotkin wrote.[379] "The governor, most recently in *Newsweek*, has cast himself as both the Subcomandante Zero of the anti-Trump resistance and savior of the planet. But when Brown finally departs Sacramento next year, he will be leaving behind a state that is in danger of falling apart both physically and socially."[380]

By contrast, Jerry Brown's father, Governor Pat Brown, left a legacy of building expansive infrastructure projects: the California State Water Project, the historical aqueduct, and more than one thousand miles of freeway. The senior Brown added three new University of California campuses and six state colleges, and many new two-year community colleges were funded.[381]

Yet today, Interstate 5, the main north–south superhighway in the state, is still mostly the same four-lane highway in most of the state, thanks to Jerry Brown, who halted construction on it in many locations. "His son is driving a stake through the heart of that very California Dream," Kotkin wrote.[382]

THE OAKLAND BAY BRIDGE REBUILD DEBACLE

The Loma Prieta Earthquake, a massive 7.1 on the Richter scale, which caused the Oakland–San Francisco Bay Bridge to break, resulting in multiple deaths, took place almost thirty years ago.[383] Under construction for more than a decade and not completed until about twenty-five years after the earthquake, the refitting and construction of a replacement span on the Bay Bridge not only took much longer than planned, but cost overruns escalated the total cost to build it to a whopping $6.4 billion. And that's not the half of it.[384]

It took a retired Bechtel metallurgist to expose Caltrans engineers as incompetent, noting they "were ignorant to the threat of hydrogen embrittle-ment—a process in which high strength metals, such as steel, become brittle and fracture due to hydrogen exposure."[385] He said Caltrans "fell on its face."

Anchor bolts meant to secure seismic equipment on the new bridge broke, attributed mainly to water-induced corrosion. "Caltrans similarly failed to take basic precautions to protect many skyway tendons from water even after the agency completed its study," the *Sacramento Bee* reported. "Those lapses and others, said nine leading experts in the corrosion of bridge tendons, intro-duced uncertainty about the durability of the skyway."[386]

DELTA WATER TUNNELS

Brown also wants two tunnels to move Northern California's water to the Central Valley and Southern California. The cost is estimated at $15 billion, but many say it will likely be over $50 billion. The fight has been big between Delta farm and property owners, environmentalists, and Brown. Opponents fear the $15+ billion, 35-mile, twin-tunnel construction project would destroy local waterways, hurt local boating and recreation, and ruin the water-based economy, home values, and the culture of the delta. They also worry that taking more freshwater out of the northern delta will increase salinity, toxin levels, and algal blooms.[387]

In 1982, when Brown was in his second term as governor, California had a statewide referendum known as the Peripheral Canal Act that would have authorized building a canal around the periphery of the Sacramento–San Joaquin River Delta to move water from Northern California down to Central and Southern California. The referendum failed.[388] The estimated cost of the Peripheral Canal in 1982 was $1 billion.

In drought-stricken California, the populous south desperately needs more water. Yet water-storage efforts have been routinely hampered by environmentalists, with no major dams being built in decades. What is needed is more water storage and a better way to distribute water throughout the state—like the delta water project.

Brown does appear to have an ally in the Trump administration on the delta water project. In June 2017, agencies of the administration, including the US Fish and Wildlife Service and the National Marine Fisheries Service, concluded that the construction of the Delta tunnel would not jeopardize endangered species, thus giving a green light to the project, one that the Obama administration had been unwilling to rule on.[389]

Historical Water Wars

California's competition over water between the northern and southern regions of the state began as conflicts between the city of Los Angeles and farmers and ranchers in Owens Valley.[390] The answer was the California Aqueduct, constructed and finished in 1913. But that was when the real fight began—over water rights.[391]

The longtime political dispute between California farmers and state and federal water regulators predates the most recent drought and will continue long after, unless some political honesty takes place.[392] By focusing on worn-out political balderdash, many in politics and the media have bypassed sincere analysis of the drought, the causes, long-standing battles, and long-term ramifications.[393]

A more realistic cause for the drought can be found in natural climate change, California's growing population, and the state's neglected water infrastructure. Also at issue are some older water-management practices in agricultural, commercial, industrial, and residential water-delivery systems—all very important influences underlying the state's current water dilemma.[394]

Most of the media and public officials paint California farmers and ranchers as the biggest water wasters in the state. Yet California's farmers and ranchers have made huge strides in improving efficient water management over the decades—it's in their best interest to do so, not only economically but also to save and conserve natural resources. Farmers and ranchers are some of the best, most efficient, and most effective conservationists California has.[395] However, hundreds of thousands of acres of California farmland were not planted in recent years because of problems with water.[396]

The last year that a dam was built in California was in 1959—when Jerry Brown's father was governor.[397] The state of California hasn't significantly invested in water storage since the 1970s when Jerry was governor the first time around.[398] "This is an era of limits and we all had better get used to it," Brown said upon being elected governor in 1975, embracing the "small is beautiful" way of thinking. Since then, California's population has doubled, as have environmental regulations and demands.[399]

The truth is that much of the state's water resources are allowed to flow out the San Francisco Bay to the Pacific Ocean for environmental purposes. Of the rest of the water, only about 10 percent goes to "urban" uses for homes and businesses, and 40 percent is used by agriculture. A full 50 percent of the water is used for environmental purposes.[400]

Trump promised California farmers he would "start opening up the water."[401] Heavy rains during 2016/2017 temporarily lightened the severity of the water problem for Californians, but longtime farmers, such as Aubrey Bettencourt of the Central Valley's pro-agriculture California Water Alliance, don't quite look to Sacramento and Brown and the liberal Democrats to lead in water policy in the state; rather, they feel they have an ally in the White House.[402]

JERRY BROWN'S HIGH-SPEED EXPRESS

The one big infrastructure project Jerry Brown has focused on, almost obsessively, is his futile high-speed-rail project. Ironically, in his previous terms as governor, Brown killed large-scale infrastructure projects, claiming, "less is more." Maturity may have changed Brown's outlook. "At this stage, as I see many of my friends dying—I went to the funeral of my best friend a couple of weeks ago—I want to get s--- done," Brown said in 2012.[403]

Brown signed into law $3 billion in construction financing for the first part of the train project, a 130-mile stretch of track—not between major urban areas as the original Proposition 1A bond voted on by the people called for, but from Bakersfield to Madera, in the Central Valley.[404] Locals began calling the train the "Conjugal Express" because it would travel between two Central Valley prison towns.

Passed by California voters in 2008, Proposition 1A, the High-Speed Rail Act of 2008, authorized the state to issue $9.95 billion in general obligation bonds and expend the funds for the construction of a 520-mile high-speed-rail system between San Francisco and Los Angeles/Anaheim.[405] Proposition 1A also restricts the High-Speed Rail Authority from spending any federal funds unless matching state funds are immediately available.[406]

Voters were assured the only cost to the state's General Fund would be to pay bond principal and interest.[407] The original price tag of $33 billion escalated to $98.5–$117 billion. Under widespread criticism, the High-Speed Rail Authority magically dropped the cost estimate to $68 billion.[408] Regardless, critics say that is just the financial launching point for only one leg of the system from Bakersfield to Fresno, and costs can and will escalate.

NOT MUCH ACCOUNTABILITY FOR BILLION-DOLLAR RAIL BOONDOGGLE

A high-speed-rail accountability measure unanimously approved by both houses of the California Legislature in 2016 was killed in the Assembly Transportation Committee later, in a 7-4 vote.[409] Assembly Bill (AB) 66 would have implemented two recommendations made by the nonpartisan Legislative

Analyst's Office to strengthen oversight of the High-Speed Rail Authority (HSRA).[410] "This vote is a slap in the face to Californians who are demanding answers about a project that is clearly in free-fall," said Assemblyman Jim Patterson, R-Fresno, author of AB 66. "They are over budget, behind schedule and are shedding project managers left and right. Democrats in California have given up their responsibility to provide oversight for high-speed rail and are now responsible for running the biggest public works scam in the country."[411]

The bill would have required the HSRA to provide more detailed information about the cost, scope, and schedule of each project segment to make it easier to track frequent changes. It would have also required business plans to include the financing costs associated with the planned system and construction of the various segments.[412]

There were several attempts by Republican lawmakers to put the measure back before the state's voters because the price to build the high-speed-rail system escalated exponentially, fare estimates doubled, and building the first segment of the train between Bakersfield and Fresno would not benefit the state's overall transportation system, according to a report done in 2012 by the California Legislative Analyst's Office (LAO).[413]

Additionally, the LAO report suggested that previous financial assumptions were too generous and that the rail project would actually require operating subsidies from the state government, which "would be contrary to explicit provisions in Proposition 1A."[414]

In 2013, State Superior Court Judge Michael Kenny ruled that the HSRA had not yet met the legal requirements to spend Proposition 1A bond funds for high-speed-rail construction.[415] In its October 11, 2013, response, the HSRA did not dispute this finding but argued that even if it could not access or spend Proposition 1A bond funds, it could proceed with construction using federal funds.[416]

In a show of unrestrained hubris and contempt, the HSRA argued that other sources of state funds, including the state's General Fund, could be used to match the federal funds.[417] This course of action would enable the HSRA to obligate the state to provide more than $3 billion in state resources toward high-speed-rail construction that might otherwise be designated for purposes, such as education, health care, or public safety, without any prior review or approval by the legislature.

In November 2013, the judge said the HSRA could not use Proposition 1A funds that were approved by the legislature in 2012. The judge denied a request by the HSRA to validate the sale of $9.9 billion in Proposition 1A bonds, determining there was no evidence that it was "necessary or desirable" to issue the bonds at that time.[418]

In February 2017, California's fourteen congressional Republicans asked Trump's Transportation Secretary Elaine Chao to block a $647 million in federal grant money from the Federal Transit Administration that the state wants to use to electrify a portion of the Caltrain commuter rail that runs between San Francisco and San Jose. Republicans said the money, which would come on top of more than $3.5 billion in federal funding already granted for construction costs, would be wasted.[419] "We think providing additional funding at this time…would be an irresponsible use of taxpayer dollars," the Republicans wrote. "The letter was spearheaded by Rep. Jeff Denham, R-Turlock, who chairs the House Transportation and Infrastructure subcommittee that oversees railroads. The Republicans also asked Chao to begin an audit of the project," *The Hill* reported.[420]

But in what was termed a "stunning reversal," the Federal Transit Administration approved the grant in May. Trump critics in the state were almost speechless. "I did not predict this," said San Jose Democrat Mayor Sam Licardo, a Trump opponent. "This is a win for everyone involved," said US Senator Dianne Feinstein.[421]

Cooperation between Washington, DC, and Sacramento Is Essential

Polls tell us that even in California, where Hillary Clinton won the presidential election by a wide margin, voters really do want to see their leaders work with Donald Trump. A UC Berkeley Institute of Government Studies poll found that 53 percent of voters believe that their mostly Democrat officeholders should try to collaborate with Trump rather than resist him at every turn.[422] Given California's huge infrastructure needs and tendency toward natural disasters, there is every reason for California voters to be concerned that their liberal politicians do not go so far off the rails in gratuitously opposing Trump that the state becomes hurt in some way. Nearly half the land in California is federally owned.[423] For example, California agencies fight wildfires on these lands, and these agencies routinely seek millions of dollars from the federal government to offset costs. This relationship is illustrative of the natural cooperation and give-and-take between agencies that support transportation, highways, and port facilities, all involving the exchange of millions and billions of taxpayer funds. Infrastructure, of all the issues facing California, is one where the feigned political drama had best be set aside for the good of the public's safety. Will California's liberal leaders be able to rise above their political grandstanding on Trump for the good of the state on infrastructure?

Only time, and still-crumbling roads and dams, will tell.

California's Education Battleground

● ● ●

PRESIDENT TRUMP'S FUNDAMENTAL APPROACH TO education policy was declared on his campaign website with this point under key issues: "We spend more per student than almost any other major country in the world. Yet, our students perform near the bottom of the pack for major advanced countries."[424]

One could say the same thing about California, where students score consistently lower than children from other states on standardized tests, and where the California Teachers Association has ensured that public school teachers in the state are among the highest paid in the nation.

Trump frequently echoed this point on the campaign trail, stating that the current system wasn't working and noting that his intention as president would be to address the problem by initiating a shift in federal education support for "school choice," allowing states to have the option to initiate voucher programs, working to "ensure universities are making a good faith effort to reduce the cost of college," and also supporting access to trade schools.

Trump's education policies likely resonated with many voters across the nation who would like to see education reform and feel schools are failing their children. Yet, his issues put him squarely on the battlefield with one of the most powerful teachers' union organizations in California and in the nation: the California Teachers Association (CTA). On the eve of Trump's inauguration, hundreds of teachers and community activists marched in protest in Los Angeles, with CTA President Eric Heins and National Education Association President Lily Eskelsen Garcia singing, "This Land Is Your Land." Their aim in the protest was to "protect public schools" in California and to send a message to Congress to reject the nomination of Betsy DeVos, Trump's selection for secretary of the US Department of Education.[425]

Federal education funding, expansion or contraction of charter schools and voucher programs, Common Core, standardized testing, California's highly paid teachers and low-performing students, the dominance of the powerful CTA, and the continuing politicization of education by California's liberal lawmakers are all at issue in potential changes the Trump administration may bring to education in California.

TRUMP'S SECRETARY OF EDUCATION

According to a profile in *Cosmopolitan*, Betsy DeVos, fifty-nine, is a "billionaire Republican donor [who] has been trying to make school vouchers a national reality for decades."[426] From Michigan, a key state in Trump's victory that he was not expected to win, she has been an active member of the Republican Party since her youth. She is a devout Christian who attended private schools, Calvin College, and Holland Christian High School, and she has been a philanthropist for conservative causes. According to *Cosmopolitan*, her primary cause has been promoting "educational choice."[427]

DeVos was hardly a surprise pick for Secretary of Education given his expressed support for school choice and vouchers. "Trump's pick for Education Secretary could put school vouchers back on the map," one headline screamed. *Education Week* reported that the Trump administration would likely pursue some type of a national school-choice policy, modeled on Florida's robust tax-credit scholarship program, which offers tax credits to entice businesses and individuals to donate to a scholarship-granting organization.[428] Opponents in the education establishment immediately claimed that a Trump/DeVos voucher plan would leave students "vulnerable to discriminatory practices, remove critical civil rights protections, and drain funding from public schools."[429] Yet at her confirmation hearing, DeVos said she wouldn't try to force states to adopt private school voucher programs,[430] and although the teachers' unions wanted to see the statement as a pullback, it was consistent with Trump's stated view to "give states the option" on vouchers.

Despite news reports claiming she had a hand in Detroit's education problems,[431] DeVos is credited with being one of the pioneers of the most successful charter school movements in the nation, leading to significant student achievement. In 2000, DeVos founded the Great Lakes Education Project, a nonprofit and advocacy group that advances school choice.[432] Nevertheless, the *Los Angeles Times* opined, "Foes fear vouchers will destroy traditional public schools and erode the separation of church and state. And there are questions about regulations: Private schools aren't required to offer bilingual education, classes for English learners or the same level of services as public schools for students with disabilities."[433]

During her Senate confirmation hearing, DeVos asked, "[w]hy, in 2017, are we still questioning parents' ability to exercise educational choice for their children?" DeVos further stated, "I am a firm believer that parents should be empowered to choose the learning environment that's best for each of their individual children."[434] CTA President Eric Heins demonstrated his union's hostility: "It seems clear to us that she is an anti–public education activist more interested in funneling public monies into private schools and for-profit charter schools," he said. "She doesn't value the diversity we celebrate and hold dear here in California." Yet critics say such obsessive focus on "diversity" in California schools has replaced academics and helped cause a downturn in student proficiency.[435]

On its website, the United Teachers of Los Angeles union (UTLA) accused the Trump administration of racism and bigotry. "Throngs of parents, students, educators, and community members throughout LAUSD [Los Angeles Unified School District] took to Twitter and the streets on January 19 to shield our schools from racism, privatization, anti-immigrant rhetoric, and destructive proposals coming from the Trump administration," UTLA said. "The protests took place one day after a Senate confirmation hearing for Secretary of Education nominee and billionaire privatizer Betsy DeVos. DeVos has never attended a public school, nor taught at one, and has worked the last two decades to defund and dismantle public education in her home state of Michigan."[436] UTLA held protests leading up to Inauguration Day in which teachers, parents, and students held signs claiming DeVos and President Trump practiced racism, sexism, and privatization.[437]

Despite the hostility and hysteria from teachers' unions, DeVos was narrowly confirmed by the Senate—but only after a historic tie-breaking vote cast by Vice President Mike Pence in his largely ceremonial role as president of the Senate.[438]

California's "Secretary of Education"

The California Department of Education is a huge state agency that spends over $76.6 billion annually when federal funds are included, overseeing public education in California.[439] It is headed by a "nonpartisan" State Superintendent of Public Instruction, currently Tom Torlakson, a former high school teacher turned politician and a former liberal Democrat member of the California State Legislature[440] who was heavily supported in his election by campaign contributions from the California Teachers Association. In fact, the CTA spent well over a staggering $13 million on Torlakson's reelection campaign against charter schools advocate Marshall Tuck in 2014.[441] Torlakson has been called a "close ally" of the teachers' union.[442]

Immediately following the election of Trump, Torlakson took to the airwaves to "reassure" California's public school students that they would be protected from discrimination and bullying.[443] "I know that the outcome of the recent Presidential election has caused deep concern among many students and their families," Torlakson said in a statement issued November 10, 2016. "The nation maintains a strong tradition for the peaceful transition of power. And I want to let all of California's 6.2 million public school students know that keeping them safe from discrimination and bullying at our great state's 11,000 public schools is a top priority."[444] Torlakson's grandstanding at Trump's expense was disingenuous, especially given statements by Immigration and Customs Enforcement officials, who have repeatedly said that "concerns about possible...ICE operations occurring on school property are unfounded" and that their policy is not to carry out enforcement actions at schools or churches, unless there is an emergency, such as a risk to human life."[445]

Torlakson was vociferously critical of the Trump administration's proposed education funding cuts, despite the governor and state legislature passing their own $2.1 billion K–12 education spending increase in 2017 from the previous year, amounting to an increase of $300 per pupil, according to Torlakson's office.[446] But that money hasn't made it and will not make it into the classrooms for California school kids. California's school districts increased spending on administrator pay faster than teacher pay, a *Sacramento Bee* review of state financial data found. Teachers all over the state argue that school districts spend a disproportionate share of available funding to pay administrators in the central offices rather than teachers.[447]

California ranked forty-first in the nation for per-pupil spending in 2013, the most recent year for which data are available, but the ranking is illusive, largely because broader education spending doesn't trickle down to the classroom.[448] However, the elephant in the room is dramatically rising pension costs.[449] Any increases in California education funding are usually siphoned off by administrator pay, teacher pay, and increasing pension costs. California ranks among the highest in teacher salaries in the nation, according to the California Department of Education (CDE). The CDE reports that the average teacher and some credentialed staff salary has grown 10.6 percent since 2014.[450]

According to projections by the nonpartisan Legislative Analyst's Office, school districts will pay $3.1 billion more to the pension system in the 2019–2020 fiscal year than they do today, whereas the minimum school budget is projected to be about $8.3 billion higher in that same year.[451] And compounding matters, school districts are not required to tell the state how they spend their money.[452]

Torlakson vowed to fight the Trump administration on numerous policy decisions, including the White House decision to rescind protections for transgender public school students. Torlakson said the change in administrations does not affect existing California law. In a press release, Torlakson reiterated his support for the rights of transgender students and reminded all Californians that state law requires public schools to allow students access to the restroom or locker room consistent with their own gender identity.[453]

California's K–12 public schools currently receive more than $7 billion annually from the federal government. The budget plan President Trump proposed would cut at least 6 percent of those funds for California. "I give this budget an 'F' grade for failing public school students in California," said Torlakson.[454] Trump's education proposal argues for a $9.2 billion net cut for the federal Department of Education, in an effort to stem the $20 trillion federal deficit.[455] The administration's cut would amount to just $400 million of the California education agency's $76.6 billion total in annual spending.[456]

Mindful of the federal education contributions to California, Torlakson filed a brief in the US Ninth District Court in support of Santa Clara County's request in February for a preliminary injunction to halt Trump's order that threatens to stop federal funding to sanctuary jurisdictions.[457] Torlakson's brief claims that the Trump order is unconstitutional because it doesn't define "sanctuary" and forces local agencies, including schools, to enforce federal immigration laws. "The Executive Order places schools, school districts and county offices of education, who have merely identified themselves as safe havens for undocumented students, in the precarious position of losing large amounts of federal funds without warning, notice or clear guidance about what is meant by the order," Torlakson said.[458]

CALIFORNIA'S LOW-PERFORMING STUDENTS AND TOP-PAID TEACHERS

In his forthcoming book, *The Corrupt Classroom: Bias, Indoctrination, Violence, Social Engineering and Other Classroom Horrors*, Izumi explains the dismal state of California's public education system and the factors contributing to such low proficiency—for example:[459]

* California eighth graders declined in reading and math skills from 2013 to 2015.
* Seventy-two percent of California eighth graders failed to achieve proficiency on the 2015 National Assessment of Educational Progress eighth-grade reading exam, and 84 percent of African American and 82 percent of Latino eighth graders failed to hit proficiency.
* On the math exam, 73 percent of California eighth graders overall, 86 percent of African Americans, and 87 percent of Latinos failed to achieve proficiency.[460]

California's decline can be attributed partly to the concurrent imposition of curricula aligned with the Common Core national education standards, according to Izumi. But the problem isn't just a bad curriculum issue and low student achievement; Izumi said that with unsafe school environments, social engineering, and politicized teachers, California parents want an exit ticket for their children out of the state's public schools—and school vouchers offer parents a viable option.[461]

Despite the criticism of the Common Core, comparative California students' performances on state-specific standardized testing based on its learning goals reveal big problems in how California teachers are delivering education. There is a large gap in meeting basic standards for black students, who only met English standards at a 31 percent rate and math standards at an 18 percent rate, whereas Asian students met the same standards at a 73 percent rate and a 67 percent rate, respectively.[462]

Rather than address the problem of failing students, the Los Angeles Unified School District (LAUSD) Board of Directors unanimously agreed to just lower the graduation requirements. In 2015, it determined that students with a D grade in courses required to enter the University of California and California State University could still graduate and earn a diploma. Nearly 54 percent of LAUSD's graduating class in 2014, or 20,514 students, failed to meet the prior requirements for graduation.[463]

Compared with students in other states, California students score near the bottom nationwide in math and reading. In fact, according to a CNBC News report, fourth graders in California performed worse on tests than students in every state in the union other than Nevada, New Mexico, Louisiana, Mississippi, and Alabama.[464] Many of the states where children perform better on standardized tests than do California kids spend far less on teacher pay than does California, where at more than $84,000 a year on average, teachers are the best paid in the nation.[465]

SECRETARY DEVOS AND SUPPORT FOR SCHOOL-CHOICE VOUCHERS

Secretary Betsy DeVos has long supported school vouchers as a way to give parents more choices in their children's education.[466] And Californians tend to agree with her. A recent poll by the Public Policy Institute of California found that a large majority of Californians support school-choice vouchers. Of the 60 percent of adults and 66 percent of public school parents who favored vouchers, African Americans and Latinos favored vouchers at even higher levels, at 73 percent and 69 percent, respectively.[467]

The reason for vouchers' popularity can be found in the fact that they grant parents public funding choices to pay for private school tuition for their children. The California Teachers Association and National Education Association strongly oppose vouchers. They see vouchers as a threat to public schools and public school teachers. They believe:

Vouchers do nothing to insure that all children are granted this most fundamental right. Not only do they divert public tax dollars to private schools that are not held accountable to the public, but they also do nothing to improve the education of the few children who receive a voucher. And they also do nothing for the majority of students who remain in public schools that are harmed by the budget cuts required to fund the vouchers.[468]

Do school vouchers improve education results? A Stanford University professor would like people to think they do not. "The evidence is very weak that vouchers produce significant gains in learning," according to Martin Carnoy at the Graduate School of Education.[469] The *New York Times* refers to "dismal results" from voucher programs.[470] Yet scholarly research supports that private school vouchers greatly improved student achievement in math and reading in the heavily low-income and minority-represented Milwaukee school system.[471] In fact, when vouchers are made available for use at private schools, the competition that is introduced for public school students' test scores improves education results in the public schools too, according to other scholarly research on Florida's system.[472]

A Trump administration voucher plan "would face huge obstacles in California" according to EdSource, which monitors California education issues.[473] The CTA mounted successful opposition campaigns, and the state has voted down two separate initiatives for school voucher programs, one in 1993[474] defeated by 69.5 to 30.4 percent, and another in 2000[475] that lost by an even wider margin. The biggest political lobby in California by far,[476] the CTA has been outright hostile to school voucher programs, which the union deems a threat to its public school monopolies.[477] California's liberal politicians' very significant opposition to vouchers and the issue's lack of traction at the polls in the state mean that any Trump administration effort to add vouchers to parent tools in favor of school choice will get nowhere in the Golden State.

CHARTER SCHOOLS

Charter schools are public schools of choice, meaning families choose them for their children. They operate with freedom from the many regulations imposed upon public schools, and they are accountable for the academic results and the promises they make in their charters.[478] Acceptance of charter schools is a different story in California than voucher programs. Parents seem to like the schools, and voters have started to accept them as well. "Los Angeles Unified School District recently experienced a huge earthquake—a political seismic shift—when school board candidates supportive of charter schools defeated incumbents backed by the powerful local teachers union," Lance Izumi, the education expert, said. "And in a one-two punch, new research shows that charter schools are improving the achievement of the predominantly minority and low-income students the District serves."[479]

Reform-backed candidates swept the LAUSD board election in May 2017. The union-backed board president lost his reelection, swinging the balance of the board toward a reform majority for the first time since 2010.[480] The election pitted the teachers' union against charter school and school-choice advocates. The reformers vowed to "fight to end seniority-based protections and pay, close struggling schools, and give families more school choices."[481]

Indeed, charter schools have been embraced by some Democrat politicians in the state who see the need for reform, including Gloria Romero, a former Democrat state senator from Los Angeles. According to Romero, "[i]ndependent research has shown time and again that charter school students perform better academically than their traditional school peers."[482] In 2014, California led the nation in the number of new charters and students served, adding 104 schools and serving 48,000 new students;[483] according to the California

Charter Schools Association, there were 1,254 charter schools in the state in 2015, the most in any state, serving over 580,000 students.[484]

In a speech to the National Alliance for Public Charter Schools, DeVos made the case for "more quality options" for children's education.[485] DeVos spoke out in favor of reducing red tape in establishing more charter schools and said:

> Today we have a great opportunity. While some of you have criticized the President's budget—which you have every right to do—it's important to remember that our budget proposal supports the greatest expansion of public school choice in the history of the United States. It significantly increases support for the Charter School Program, and adds an additional $1 billion for public school choice for states that choose to adopt it.[486]

Most significant in DeVos's speech was a statement that "we do not need 500 page charters." DeVos's statement reveals an understanding that efforts by opponents to undermine or derail the expansion of charter schools will focus on making them more and more subject to the regulatory constraints—labor rules and otherwise—that have made public schools less successful. California supporters of the charter school movement therefore appear to have a strong, understanding ally in Trump's Department of Education.

COMMON CORE CONTROVERSY

While on the campaign trail, Trump talked about dismantling the federal Department of Education and said Common Core was a "disaster."[487] Common Core is a set of national math and English standards, which most states, including California, have adopted. The idea behind Common Core is to introduce "critical thinking" and standard goals on what a student should know and be able to do at the end of a grade.[488] Common Core is intended to establish a standard test regime in order to evaluate and compare student achievement and learn more about improving the delivery of education, ideally to be used to evaluate teacher performance and improve accountability.

Critics of Common Core, including Izumi at the Pacific Research Institute, object to how the plan is implemented. Izumi argues from his observation that the cooperative team learning associated with the plan can lead to unequal participation among team members, with the more advanced students being more involved and carrying most of the work, and that groups might not work at an even and complete pace,[489] thus hurting overall student achievement. He feels California should have its own, different testing standards than Common Core.

Although it is up to each state to set its own educational standards, and the federal government does not mandate a uniform national standard, some believe Common Core has been adopted in a number of states because of the funding incentives and influence applied by the Obama administration,[490] which supported the effort, along with rank-and-file teachers' union members. However, other supporters of Common Core included Republican Jeb Bush; education reform advocate Michelle Rhee, formerly the District of Columbia public school chancellor and now of California; and several GOP governors,[491] including Ohio Governor John Kasich. Even DeVos has been a supporter of groups that have championed Common Core.[492]

Opponents of the Common Core have included Republican Senators Lindsey Graham and Charles Grassley and the Heritage Foundation; these opponents have accused the Obama administration of "strong-arming" the forty-five states that adopted the standards into accepting it.[493] Even California's liberal state government has opposed aspects of the plan and worked to obtain a waiver from full implementation of Common Core in California over the issue of teacher accountability. A rational aspect of Common Core is to use the results of standardized testing by incorporating the data into teacher evaluations, to make teachers associated with poorly performing students more accountable.[494] California's education lobby, dominated by the CTA union, doesn't like that idea of accountability.

DeVos has been criticized for supporting Common Core prior to her nomination as Secretary of Education. "Michigan parents have tried for years to eliminate Common Core, only to be opposed at every turn by DeVos and the organizations she founded and led," wrote Jane Robbins with Truth in American Education. "And although she now claims she's 'not a supporter' of the national standards, any education activist in Michigan can tell you she certainly was a supporter—and an effective one—in the very recent past."[495]

Yet DeVos has since said she is not a supporter, and as secretary, she gave Fox News the following response when asked if she would withhold federal funds to states that decide to maintain Common Core standards:

> There isn't really any Common Core anymore. Each state is able to set the standards for their state. They may elect to adopt very high standards for their students to aspire to and to work toward. And that will be up to each state."[496]

In saying that each state "is able to set the standards for their state," DeVos is articulating a policy derived from what Trump repeated again and again on the campaign trail—that one national standard as embodied in Common Core would not be imposed by his administration. For California, whether the state has adopted Common Core standards or not, it is certain that the Trump administration will not condition federal funding on forcing California to adopt or change its standards—the way the Obama administration had operated.

HIGHER EDUCATION INTOLERANCE

Colleges across the country have seen an increase in political activism since the election, and this is especially the case at the University of California, which has seen rejection of free-speech rights for conservatives and Republicans, rioting, property damage, and student harassment and assaults when a contrasting view has attempted to present itself on campus. Demands of segregation are becoming commonplace on college campuses, and free speech is "missing in action" on these campuses.[497]

At UC Berkeley, riots followed Trump's election. When conservatives were scheduled to speak on campus, ultra-leftist Berkeley Mayor Jesse Arreguin told local police to stand down against violence that was not immediately life threatening, with a result that left conservative demonstrators pummeled for their attempt at free expression.[498] When fights, violence, arson, and extensive property destruction broke out over the speaking invitation of Breitbart editor Milo Yiannopoulos, police were reportedly hiding inside buildings and on balconies while rioters committed mayhem.[499] Predictably, Mayor Arreguin, a supporter of the leftist "By Any Means Necessary" organization, blamed conservatives for the riots.[500]

Students attending Yiannopoulos's speech were attacked with rocks, bottles, and bricks; they were pepper sprayed, and someone was beaten unconscious by the rioting thugs. "When asked why police didn't move in and stop the rioters, UC Berkeley spokesperson Dan Mogulof curiously said, 'Police tactics are driven on a campus by need, the non-negotiable need to protect our students and ensure their well-being,'" one television station reported. "University officials said police decided to stay back to prevent injuring innocent protesters and bystanders who could have been hurt if officers waded into the crowd."[501] Several sources reported that a stand-down order was issued to UC police, just as had been done at UC Davis three weeks earlier at another Milo event, which also turned violent.[502]

Two months later, another "resist" event occurred at UC Berkeley when conservative speaker Ann Coulter was scheduled to speak at the invitation of the College Republicans and Young America's Foundation (YAF).[503] The YAF requested that UC Berkeley treat Coulter the same way liberal speakers were treated: provide proper protections, including a "zero-tolerance" policy for disruptors and police protection, but to no avail. YAF ended up canceling support for Coulter's speech because UC Berkeley officials would not offer protections for attendees.[504] "Berkeley made it impossible to hold a lecture due to the lack of assurances for protections from foreseeable violence from unrestrained leftist agitators," YAF staff wrote.[505]

Following the rioting after Yiannopoulos's scheduled and canceled appearance at UC Berkeley, President Trump sent out a Tweet questioning whether Berkeley should continue to receive federal funding.[506] And for good reason—universities and colleges are supposed to be bastions of ideas and learning, especially UC Berkeley, the historic center of the "free-speech" movement started by activist Mario Savio in 1964 during the Vietnam War.[507]

CALIFORNIA'S CORRUPTED UNIVERSITY SYSTEM

As a candidate, Trump said the cost of college tuition and debt could go down if universities would make an effort to reduce costs in exchange for federal tax dollars. California is, unfortunately, an example of a university system that is doing the opposite of Trump's vision. A recent state audit established that University of California President Janet Napolitano's office essentially hid $175 million in reserves, padding the salaries and benefits of her staff and creating a budget without accounting for the hidden reserves.[508]

"The UC Board of Regents just raised tuition on students and has nearly doubled in-state student tuition over the last 10 years, while spending hundreds of millions of dollars on projects and administrative salaries," State Auditor Elaine Howle said in her audit. "Students and their families deserve confidence that their money is being spent wisely. The UC Office of the President acknowledges the need to address the Auditor's findings. I look forward to working with my Assembly colleagues, students, and the UC to get to the bottom of this and do all we can to help UC get its financial house in order."[509]

The auditor also accused Napolitano's office of intercepting a confidential survey that the auditor sent to individual campuses about the quality and cost of services they received from the central office, causing campus officials to soften their responses. Howle said that the UC Office of the President interfered by reviewing the surveys sent independently to the UC's ten campus leaders and changing answers to reflect more positively on UC's operations.[510]

Napolitano is no stranger to politics or to the demands of transparency in public office. She served as the Democrat Governor of Arizona and Obama's Secretary of Homeland Security. Napolitano should be on the same wavelength with California's liberal leaders: as Secretary of Homeland Security, she took actions to eliminate the word "terrorism" from the department's official lexicon as part of an agenda to "understand" and "reflect" grievances of Muslim communities.[511] Yet for years, Democrat state lawmakers have been clashing with the university system over its opaque finances and escalating costs amid calls for belt-tightening by Governor Brown. Tension between the state and the prestigious university system has mounted since the recession, when UC repeatedly hiked tuition to backfill state budget cuts and turned away record numbers of California high school seniors while admitting higher-paying, out-of-state and international students.

"In my 17 years as state auditor, we have never had a situation like this," Howle said.[512] Trump's call for colleges and universities to control costs as a means to lower the cost of college for students seemed lost on the UC system, which did not announce an end to what news outlets reported as "lavish spending on dinners" for board members and staff until the state audit.[513] Napolitano reimbursed UC Regents more than $225,000 for dinner parties, including a $17,600 banquet held the night before the board voted to raise tuition.[514]

POLITICIZATION OF EDUCATION

Yvette Felarca, a middle school social studies teacher at Martin Luther King Jr. Middle School, attended a protest against Milo Yiannopoulos's scheduled speech at UC Berkeley. In a rant while at the Berkeley protest, Felarca reportedly called on protesters to prevent Yiannopoulos from speaking "by any means necessary." Felarca is also the leader of the radical "By Any Means Necessary" organization, or BAMN, which the *San Jose Mercury News* described "as a 'militant' group that uses a variety of tactics, including violence, to spread its message." BAMN says, "Trump must go, by any means necessary."[515]

A video of Felarca's rage was posted to YouTube but has since been removed. However, several news organizations were at the protest and reported what Felarca said:

"This is not about free speech," Felarca said of Yiannopoulos' Dangerous Faggot Tour. "These are not people who are interested in any genuine debate. They hide behind that hypocritically to try to shut up and put in our places women or Muslims or minorities or oppressed groups. But what they are really trying to do is they're trying to assert their power, threaten us, intimidate us, rape us, kill us.

"This is real. This is life and death. This is not an abstract question of who's theory are you interested in researching. This is about our lives right now…

"I promise you, if we work together and we stay united, we can count on each other. We can shut this f***er down, we can get rid of Trump," she continued. "I know it, and when the Nazis tried to kill some of us, after we recovered, some of them threatened me and students at my school and tried to get me fired. But they didn't succeed, and the students and the parents and the community rallied together and not only got me my job back but we're stronger now, so we have got to stay united."[516]

Felarca ordered dozens of other radical leftists to converge on campus and shut down Yiannopoulos's free-speech tour "by any means necessary." California teachers' union members joined the protest.

FEDERAL FUNDING AND BROWN'S LOCAL CONTROL FUNDING FORMULA
Despite being accused of taking a "meat-cleaver" to federal education spending by Randi Weingarten, American Federation of Teachers union president,[517] the Trump administration appears most focused on plans to return the power and authority to states, local officials, and parents. "That smart move alone will force state and local leaders to do what state and local had been doing long before there ever was a Cabinet-level Department of Education," the *Washington Times* reported. "So cast aside the union leader's opinion. Facts speak louder than hyperbole."[518]

Whereas Trump calls for more "local control" of education, Governor Brown's signature education reform, the Local Control Funding Formula (LCFF), adopted by the state in 2013, is quite a different take on the notion. The legislation proposed a significant transfer of funds from suburban school districts to urban school districts, based solely on poverty and language.[519] The plan then adds additional funding where this particular student population exceeds 55 percent of all the students in a district. Of the six million K–12 students in the California system, more than 25 percent are English learners. The LCFF assumes that shifting billions of extra dollars from economically better-off districts will dramatically boost performance among students in districts where residents are poorer, in foster care, or where English is not the first language.[520]

According to the California Department of Education, under the LCFF, school districts receive "grade span–specific base grants" plus supplemental grants calculated on student demographic factors such as low-income status and non-English fluency. Districts have "greater flexibility to use these funds to improve student outcomes." What this means is that school districts with high ethnic student populations receive more money and attention than a district that is less ethnic and more English speaking.[521]

In his 2016 State of the State address, Brown criticized the micromanagement of educators "through increasingly minute and prescriptive state and federal regulations." With his LCFF program, he proclaimed, "California has led the country in the way it is returning control to local school districts."[522] "But simply shifting spending discretion from one level of government to another still means that government is in control of decision-making, with predictably bad results," education scholar Izumi reported.[523] Eventually, Brown admitted there is no connection between the LCFF and student outcomes. But the plan remains, just the same.[524]

Is Education Reform in Store for California?

If California's education system is to be reformed, it is not going to happen as a result of Trump's election to the presidency. Although there will be a shift in federal education support to "school choice," this will largely be seen in moral support for charter schools and opposition to California's efforts to further regulate them to take away their flexibility. Although the Trump administration likes voucher programs, it will not require California to offer this particular form of school choice, and it is highly unlikely that California's educational establishment will allow it in any event. As stated, federal funding will be continued and will not be tied to adoption of the Common Core national standards as attempted during the Obama administration, as every state will be able to adopt its own educational standards. It is possible that funding for some university and college programs will be tied to promises that those institutions will respect First Amendment rights, but there is no apparent plan to do so coming out of the Department of Education. Thus, Californian's gains for education policy with Trump's election will be limited, largely because of a resistant educational lobby that keeps the state's teachers the most highly paid and the students among the lowest performers in achievement in the nation.

California's Dangerous Medicare
Expansion under Obamacare

● ● ●

DONALD TRUMP IS NOT TO blame for California's Medicaid crisis; rather, the state's liberal politicians are to blame because they allowed for an enormous and expensive expansion of the free health-care program beyond poverty-level families that is now a noose around taxpayers' necks.

California's health-care system, like such systems in the rest of the country, relies in large part on employer-sponsored insurance. The state's total health-care spending in 2016 is estimated by UCLA to have been $367 billion, dwarfing the state's General Fund spending.[525] California's high cost of living likely contributes to the costs of medical professionals as well. The average salary of a registered nurse, for example, is $135,000, which compares to $65,000 a year under the Canadian single-payer system.[526] State and federal government spending, including the big Medicare program for seniors, accounted for 71 percent of health-care spending in 2016.[527] Medicaid, and California's version, Medi-Cal, is a free health-care program for the poor that is paid for by both federal and state contributions

CALIFORNIA'S POLITICAL GRANDSTANDING ON OBAMACARE

The current problems with and future of health care constitute a very serious issue for California. Nevertheless, it is an issue ripe with demagoguery among California's ruling elite. "No parent should worry if they can afford to take their child to a doctor or a hospital," said State Attorney General Xavier Becerra in yet another press statement lambasting Trump.[528] "President

Trump's unpredictable behavior and lack of defense of the health care coverage of millions of Americans under the ACA [Affordable Care Act] threatens to resurrect those fears of every parent," he added. Becerra was commenting on one more lawsuit he had just joined, but if he had a bone to pick, it was more with a federal district court judge than Donald Trump. Becerra was seeking to intervene in a federal lawsuit filed in 2014, when Obama was president, that successfully challenged the funding of federal payments under the ACA because they were not properly authorized by Congress. The Obama administration appealed the lawsuit, and with Trump in the White House, ACA supporters were fearful the appeal would be undermined. But it wasn't, and Trump said the subsidies would stay in place until Obamacare was resolved, a promise lost on Xavier Becerra.[529]

US Senator Kamala Harris said that GOP plans to change Obamacare "will effectively end Medicaid." But nonprofit fact-checking organization PolitiFact researched the issue and found that a Congressional Budget Office estimate on the Senate Obamacare reform bill hardly "ends" Medicaid but rather reduced the budget for the program by about 26 percent over ten years. The truth: cuts would need to be made in Medicaid spending, but the program would surely not end,[530] and Harris was grossly exaggerating the facts for the sake of heightening the political conflict.

CALIFORNIA'S COSTLY MEDICAID EXPANSION

California has been somewhat insulated from many of the more drastic problems of Obamacare that plague other states, such as sky-high premium increases, high deductibles, and lack of access to a doctor of choice.[531] However, California has a much bigger problem brought on by Obamacare. Under the ACA (Obamacare) law, the federal government enticed states to expand their own health-care programs from poverty up to lower-income residents by offering to pay 100 percent of any expansion of Medicaid in a state in the first three years, but after the third year, the states that agreed to the expansion were required to start picking up part of the tab for the cost of the expansion.

California's expansion was huge, adding close to five million[532] new enrollees to the free, government-subsidized health-care program, many of whom were not poverty-level residents but simply lower-income, able-bodied individuals well above the poverty line. These residents qualified under Obamacare's expansion to include not just poverty-level families, as in the past, but also childless adults earning up to 38 percent above the top poverty-line level.[533]

Thus, the Obamacare Medicaid expansion that was adopted by California transformed Medi-Cal from a free health-care program for families in poverty to a program that provides free health care to not just the poor but lower-income people above the poverty line, including single, able-bodied working individuals without dependents. Through 2020, California's required contribution for these new enrollees in Medi-Cal will be increased under Obamacare incrementally every year. In 2017–2018, California is expected to receive $17 billion from the federal government under Obamacare to pay for the expansion.[534] California's expansion of Medicaid through Medi-Cal will require an additional *state* expenditure of $1.3 billion in 2017, putting further strain on the state's current budget[535] and even more into the future. These funds are in addition to about $16 billion more that the state already shells out for other Medi-Cal recipients.

The *Los Angeles Times* published an op-ed piece on "California's Medi-Cal Explosion" as early as August 2014, when Obama still had a two and a half years in his term, and Donald Trump wasn't on anyone's mind as being Obama's successor. The article, by Anna Gorman, a senior correspondent at Kaiser Health News, opened by saying, "California is coming face to face with the reality of one of its biggest Obamacare successes: the explosion in Medi-Cal enrollment."[536] Gorman wrote that the high number of enrollees in the state had "surprised healthcare experts and created unforeseen challenges for state officials."[537] The overriding question was, how does the state deal with a "staggering number of Medi-Cal beneficiaries" while also improving their health and keeping costs down? Gorman cited a myriad of problems with the Medi-Cal expansion that included low beneficiary payments, lack of doctor acceptance, a state backlog in enrolling the hundreds of thousands of new applicants, and problems with high-quality delivery of services from the managed health-care providers that Medi-Cal contracts with. According to the California HealthCare Foundation, California ranked below the national average for "consumer experience," such as relationships with doctors and getting treatment quickly, although quality was on par with the rest of the nation.[538]

Yet, the same *Los Angeles Times* that published the article stating the problem editorialized glowingly about the expansion and about how the promised repeal and replacement of Obamacare by Donald Trump and congressional Republicans could negatively affect the lower-income population of Los Angeles.[539] "With expanded Medicaid, there was finally a mappable route to viability and perhaps admission to the ranks of the middle class for Los Angeles County's poor, sick, mentally ill, addicted and other living at the margins...without it...we can expect our poor neighbors to become poorer."[540] According to the *Times*, 40 percent of the county's population relies on free Medicaid for health care, and "[m]any would be at great risk of losing health coverage" if Obamacare were repealed and replaced and if Medicaid was "slashed" and "devastated" by Republicans. It was perhaps lost on the *Times* that free health care for 40 percent of the large county's population might also present some funding problems.

It was California's liberal politicians who took Obama up on his offer to initially fund a wide expansion of a free health-care program that would quickly grow to be a dangerous and costly noose around state taxpayers' necks. The financial sustainability of this program is now at risk. About fourteen million Californians are now Medi-Cal recipients, representing more than one-third of the state's population, and the total tax bill for health care for those residents is $100 billion, with nearly 66 percent of it currently paid by the federal government,[541] support that is set to diminish not just under reform by congressional Republicans but under Obamacare itself.

Although 33 percent or more of Californians now enjoy free health care under what was intended to be just a poverty program, the state's official poverty rate is 15 percent, or 20.6 percent if you include cost of living, according to the Census Bureau.[542] By either calculus of poverty, it is clear that millions of people in California who are living above the poverty rate and are able-bodied have ended up enjoying free health care in California, and these millions of better-off recipients are now threatening the cost and viability of the program for the poorer families it is intended to serve.

Comparing California to a state that did not agree to the Obamacare Medicaid expansion reveals a lot about why the expansion is a bad thing for California. Whereas California's Medi-Cal recipients number 33 percent under the expansion, Kansas's Medicaid recipients number 387,934, or just 12 percent of the population, even though this rate exceeds the poverty-level rate of 9.9 percent in Kansas when cost of living is taken into account.[543] Thus, Kansas has almost three times lower the percentage of recipients than California, and less of a financial burden on the state, even though its program is servicing a higher number of people than its poverty rate reveals.

California's huge Medicaid expansion will put further strain on an already "high-tax" state that has other problems—such as a grossly underfunded public employee pension system. The problem is even more acute because as Medi-Cal enrollment has increased, the number of doctors willing to take Medi-Cal patients has declined because of unrealistic cost controls imposed by the state.[544]

At the same time, health care beyond Medicaid must be reformed on a national level. According to a report by the Department of Health and Human Services, all thirty-nine states participating in Obamacare saw increases in individual market premiums from 2013 to 2017, contrary to President Obama's promises that premiums would not go up.[545] The average individual market premiums were up 105 percent, and Alaska, Alabama, and Oklahoma saw premiums triple.

Something has to give, and the federal commitment to Medicaid/Medi-Cal in California will likely tighten further. Advisors to Governor Brown estimate that cuts in Trump's budget proposal could cost the state an average of $1.86 billion a year over the next ten years.[546] Yet, *National Review* writes that under Republican reforms, the "vast majority of California's Medicaid recipients are unlikely to find themselves expelled from the state's rolls."[547] Republican reforms will slow the growth of Medicaid and not radically slash it; however, "it's true that a reduction in federal funding means that states will have to shoulder more burden of their own programs, and that certain states are going to struggle more than others do."[548]

California will be one of those states. The choices the state's liberal policy makers will face with Obamacare reform, who themselves in June 2017 came dangerously close to imposing an unfunded, massive $400 billion single-payer universal health-care system that would abolish private health insurance for all in the state,[549] will be to either further tax residents, now to an extreme, to cover the fiscal mistake of their Medi-Cal expansion or do the right thing and rewrite eligibility requirements. Rewritten eligibility requirements would restore the solvency of the program by reinstating it as primarily for poor families and not including able-bodied single adults without dependents, who could always get a job and resort to employee insurance or the insurance market. What do you think they will do?

Real Risks to Homeland Security in California

● ● ●

ON DECEMBER 14, 2015, IN San Bernardino at an annual training session and holiday party at the Inland Regional Center, a terrorist attack by two Islamic extremist terrorists—a husband and wife—took place. There were more than eighty county employees in attendance when fellow employee Syed Farook, twenty-eight, an environmental health specialist with the county, and his wife, Tashfeen Malik, twenty-seven, a native Pakistani who entered the country under a "K-1" fiancé visa, opened fire and turned the holiday party into a scene of horror.[550] Within two minutes, fourteen people, mostly public employees, were dead, and another twenty-two were severely injured. The FBI confirmed the attack was terrorism, plotted and carried out by the Redlands couple who associated themselves with radical Islam.[551]

Farook was a US-born citizen of Pakistani descent who worked as a San Bernardino Department of Public Health employee. Media reported that the terror attack may have been "triggered" by the Christmas holiday lunch "replete with holiday decorations, including a Christmas tree."[552]

Farook and Malik met first online, then in person on a Hajj pilgrimage to Mecca, Islam's holiest city, in Saudi Arabia on October 3, 2013.[553] They were engaged the same day, and Farook and Malik subsequently filled out a twenty-one-page application to enter the United States. The *Los Angeles Times* reported that Malik sent private messages to friends on Facebook in 2012, before her visa was granted, and in 2014,[554] after she had arrived in the United States, but these clues to the radicalization of the couple were apparently missed by the authorities.

The FBI concluded that Farook and Malik separately radicalized on the Internet as early as 2011, largely from materials posted online by Al Qaeda.[555] The two had originally planned to open fire on people at Riverside City College and attack motorists at an inescapable choke point along the 91 Freeway, Enrique Marquez Jr., told authorities.[556] Marquez was a friend of Farook and Malik. "The plans were halted in 2012 when FBI agents coincidentally arrested a group of local men who planned to join Al-Qaeda overseas and attack American service personnel there, according to an FBI affidavit filed in federal court," the *San Bernardino Sun* reported.[557]

Despite the Islamic State of Iraq and Syria (ISIS) group taking credit for the San Bernardino attack,[558] as recently as December 2016, the FBI reported that despite piecing together the couple's actions up to and including the massacre, they still don't have answers to some of the critical questions.[559] The FBI said it is still trying to determine whether anyone was aware of the couple's plot or helped them in any way.[560]

Thus, although *Time*'s headline proclaimed, "Climate Change Is the 'Mother of All Risks' to National Security" in California, experience tells us there are greater and more immediate concerns to homeland security in the nation's largest state. Domestic and foreign terrorism stand out as the first priority.[561]

Terrorism can occur in many forms. For example, California is home to major entertainment centers like Disneyland in Anaheim and SeaWorld in San Diego. Its baseball, football, basketball, and other many sports venues across the state are places large numbers of people congregate and are made vulnerable to potential terrorist attacks, such as the Boston bombing incident. Terrorism can also include hacking on the Internet. California is home to more than thirty major military installations, by far the most of any US state. Yet, "California does not yet have a major Department of Defense cybersecurity footprint," concluded Governor Brown's Military Council in its 2015 report, "Maintaining and Expanding California's National Security Mission, Report and Recommendations."[562] "However, recent announcements by DoD [Department of Defense] of a 'cybercom' point of presence in Silicon Valley are beginning to change that. In addition, the Army National Guard recently announced California as the first state to receive a new cyber unit, capable of both federal and state operations."[563] In addition, California has seen horrific terror attacks perpetrated by radical Islamic terrorists,[564] and not just in San Bernardino.

Los Angeles Metro Red Line Threat

In December 2016, the Los Angeles County Sheriff and city police received an overseas tip about an imminent bombing of the Metro Red Line's Universal City station, which has 150,000 daily boardings and connects North Hollywood with central and downtown Los Angeles.

The threat forced federal and local law enforcement in Los Angeles to swiftly ramp up security across its sprawling transit system.[565] Los Angeles Police Chief Charlie Beck said that LA law enforcement reviews threats "constantly." In light of the "very specific" nature of the threat, Chief Beck said his department did not have the time to vet the threat in the way they would have preferred because they had to move so quickly on it.[566]

Gunman in Fresno Kills Three

In April 2017, three men were shot and killed by Kori Ali Muhammad, a black gunman in Fresno.[567] The suspect yelled "Allahu Akbar," during the attack, which means "God is great" in Arabic, before he was arrested, according to Fresno Police Chief Jerry Dyer.[568] "But the Associated Press (AP)made an editorial decision to print the translation of his words from Arabic to English: 'God is great,'" Fox News reported.[569]

The AP barely corrected the glaring omission with a tweet two days later that read, "We deleted a tweet about a Fresno slaying suspect shouting 'God is great.' It failed to note he said it in Arabic. A new tweet is upcoming."[570]

Muhammad fired seventeen rounds in less than two minutes, police said.[571] He later told police that he hates white people. His victims were all Caucasian males apparently chosen at random.[572] Yet shortly after the attack, Fresno police went out of their way to call it a "racially motivated hate crime" instead of a terrorist attack.[573] However, Muhammad had a history of violent behavior that would lead most to believe this attack was related to Islam.

Between 1997 and 2004, Muhammad was accused in four cases of viciously beating women, according to Sacramento County court records.[574] "He threw her to [the] floor, threw her on [the] bed, and grabbed her hair," read the investigating officer's account of the assault on his child's mother in 1997.[575] A witness said she saw Muhammad slap the woman several times and later stomp on her head with his bare foot at least twice.[576]

LODI TERROR ATTACK

In June 2005, Hamid Hayat, a Pakistani immigrant, was arrested in Lodi, California, after allegedly lying to the FBI about his attendance at an Islamic terrorist training camp in Pakistan.[577] Hamid was found guilty of providing himself as "material support" to terrorists and three counts of providing false statements to the FBI. In interviews with the FBI, he stated (correctly) that he specifically requested to come to the United States after receiving training in order to carry out jihad. He was sentenced to twenty-four years in prison.[578]

9/11 TERRORISTS LIVED IN CALIFORNIA

On September 11, 2001, the well-known tragedy occurred: two commercial passenger jet planes crashed into the World Trade Center, and a third plane crashed into the Pentagon. A fourth plane crashed into a field after its passengers bravely tried to overcome the hijackers.

It was discovered that three of the 9/11 suicide hijackers lived in San Diego, and several more allegedly visited as they planned the attacks. But there were also many other radical Islamic terrorists in the region who assisted the terrorists.[579] A radical local Imam who counseled the hijackers, a mysterious Saudi man who funded a local mosque, and even an advance man who worked for the Saudi government, among others, were part of the plot. According to the *San Diego Union Tribune*, some were never detained or properly investigated. None was ever convicted of any crimes related to 9/11, and most have since left the country.[580]

ASSAULT ON CALIFORNIA POWER STATION: DOMESTIC TERRORISM?
California's energy grid has been compromised, and not just because politicians have facilitated the removal of nuclear power from the mix; California is vulnerable to attacks, as happened in 2013 and 2014 on a Pacific Gas & Electric (PG&E) utility substation, cutting power to thousands.[581] Such attacks could become terrorist motivated. A bizarre sniper attack in April 2013 knocked out a PG&E electrical substation near San Jose that is the source of energy for thousands of customers.[582]

The attack at the substation raised fears that the entire country's power grid is vulnerable to terrorism. "Until the Metcalf incident, attacks on US utility equipment were mostly linked to metal thieves, disgruntled employees or bored hunters, who sometimes took potshots at small transformers on utility poles to see what happens. (Answer: a small explosion followed by an outage)," the *Wall Street Journal* reported.[583]

"The attack began just before 1 a.m. on April 16 last year, when someone slipped into an underground vault not far from a busy freeway and cut telephone cables. Within half an hour, snipers opened fire on a nearby electrical substation. Shooting for 19 minutes, they surgically knocked out 17 giant transformers that funnel power to Silicon Valley. A minute before a police car arrived, the shooters disappeared into the night."

A top Department of Homeland Security official revealed in 2015 that the 2013 sniper attack on the energy grid substation may have been committed by someone on the inside. The attack was called "the most significant incident of domestic terrorism involving the grid that has ever occurred" by the nation's top electrical utility regulator.[584]

And then the same energy-grid substation was hit again sixteen months later in 2014. An unknown number of thieves cut through a fence and made off with power tools, a pipe bender, and ground compactors used to smooth out dirt after excavations, PG&E reported.[585]

The FBI said at the time that it did not consider the incident terrorism. But Jon Wellinghoff, the chief of the Federal Energy Regulatory Commission at the time, said he did believe it was a terror attack, based on the analysis of experts he brought to the crime scene. The analysis pointed to the shell casings having no fingerprints and evidence that the shooting positions had been prearranged.[586]

No arrests were made in the case. Many were critical that the attack was not further pursued by the Obama administration, or the FBI, because there were concerns it could have been a dry run for a much larger attack.[587]

CALIFORNIA PUSHING THE ENVELOPE ON WHERE THE DANGER LIES
Shortly after Trump was elected president, the San Francisco Police Department announced it was "pulling out of the FBI's Joint Terrorism Task Force, and its cutting ties."[588] "San Francisco says it doesn't want its police gathering intelligence or surveilling Muslims or anyone else involved with political protests," Fox News reported,[589] "or to keep records, and they fear that will happen illegally under President Trump."

Governor Brown went to China in early June 2017, where he held talks with Chinese President Xi Jinping and the Chinese envoy on climate change. Brown and the leaders of the world's largest Communist state signed a new climate-change agreement between the State of California and the People's Republic of China.[590,591]

Article 1, Section 10 of the US Constitution forbids states from entering "into any Treaty, Alliance, or Confederation," and says that foreign policy belongs solely to the federal government.[592]

In his State of the State address in January, Brown castigated the "climate deniers" who argue against scientific consensus and called climate change one of the greatest dangers Americans face. "The science is clear. The danger is real," Brown said.[593] Yet it seems that climate change is really the only "danger" Brown ever references.

When President Trump was headed to Hamburg, Germany, for the June G20 summit, Brown showed up one day before the G20 meetings were to begin and announced that Trump "does not speak for most Americans when it comes to dealing with environmental concerns." President Trump decided to withdraw the United States from the 2015 Paris climate accord.[594]

"Yes, I know President Trump is trying to get out of the Paris Agreement, but he doesn't speak for the rest of America," Brown said in a video message shown to tens of thousands at the Global Citizen Festival in Hamburg. "We in California and in states all across America believe it's time to act. It's time to join together, and that's why at this Climate Action Summit we're going to get it done."[595]

As for security on California's southern border with Mexico, Brown announced he would fight Trump on a border wall and immigration control. Brown likened Trump to a strongman whose goal of walling off the US–Mexico border conjures other infamous barriers from the past.[596] "The wall, to me, is ominous. It reminds me too much of the Berlin Wall," Brown said during an interview on *Meet the Press*.[597] The governor has continued to dispute Trump's stance that open border immigration is a public safety threat.[598]

President's National Security Actions

Since taking office, Trump has demonstrated how serious he is on national security with his appointments to key security positions:[599]

- **General H. R. McMaster**—National Security Advisor. McMaster served, among other posts, as Commander of the Combined Joint Inter-Agency Task Force Shafafiyat in Kabul, Afghanistan.
- **General James Mattis**—Department of Defense. Mattis is a four-star US Marine Corps general who led US Central Command from 2010 to 2013.
- **Retired General John Kelly**—Department of Homeland Security Secretary. Like Mattis, Kelly is a veteran of more than forty years in the US Marine Corps, having served as commander of the US Southern Command.

Within his first one hundred days, Trump prioritized rebuilding and empowering the military to restore national security. He advocated increasing the defense budget by $54 billion to end the devastating effects of the sequestration that has persisted for years. Trump empowered commanders in the field to make decisions, and he vowed to develop a state-of-the-art missile defense system to protect against missile-based attacks from states like Iran and North Korea.

The Trump administration also acknowledged that cyberwarfare is an emerging battlefield and is working to take measures to safeguard our national security secrets and systems. Trump vowed to prioritize the development of defensive and offensive cyber-capabilities at the US Cyber Command and to recruit the best and brightest Americans to serve in this crucial area.[600]

Trump signed an executive order to establish initial funding for the US–Mexico border wall's construction and has since received hundreds of bids for the construction of the border wall.

Finally, but not lastly, the president overturned the Obama administration policy of appeasement toward Cuba. And, in doing so, Trump promised to restore some of the restrictions on Cuba until that country provides religious and political freedom to its people.[601]

The contrasts between President Trump and Governor Brown are stark on the issue of national security. Although a governor is not in charge of national security, California has a different level of responsibility to take national security seriously, as home to the most military installations, as home of the brain trust in Silicon Valley, as a border state to Mexico, and as a Pacific Rim state. Climate change is hardly the biggest danger to residents of the state; rather, it is just a convenient obfuscation by liberal politicians when the issue of security is raised.

Which is a more serious threat: North Korea's escalating aggression and threats to launch missiles toward the West Coast of the United States or spending trillions of dollars to try to reduce planetary temperatures 0.057 degrees in fifty years or so?[602]

Whose Travel Ban?

• • •

DONALD TRUMP FULFILLED A MAJOR campaign promise to improve national security when he first ordered, on January 27, 2017, a ninety-day *temporary* suspension of the entry of foreign nationals to the United States from countries the Obama administration had recognized as terrorist-prone. "This is not about religion," Trump said in an announcement on January 29. "This is about terror and keeping our country safe. There are over 40 different countries worldwide that are majority Muslim that are not affected by this order."[603]

California's liberal leaders, such as US Senator Dianne Feinstein, were quick to seize on campaign rhetoric and label Trump's order a "Muslim ban."[604] Yet, it wasn't really a travel ban, let alone a ban on Muslims, according to the US Supreme Court's subsequent interpretation of the text of a second, similar executive order, issued on March 6. It was a temporary pause so that the nation could have time to retool its vetting procedures for national security. Ironically, California's own restriction on the use of public funds for travel to certain states because of objections to those states' treatment of gay and transgender people, such as requiring individuals to choose a public restroom that corresponds to their gender at birth, is a travel ban.

Trump's second order—Executive Order 2—temporarily suspended the entry of foreign nationals from six countries with heightened terrorism risks: Iran, Libya, Somalia, Sudan, Syria, and Yemen. Trump's previous Executive Order 1, which had included Iraq, was withdrawn after opposition in the federal court system. The new order, which was also challenged in multiple federal courts, not only included the same 90-day pause that appeared in the first order but also suspended for 120 days the nation's Refugee Admissions

Program, capped such admissions to fifty thousand annually, and provided for studies on improving processing for the national security of foreign nationals and refugees during the suspension period.[605] In considering and agreeing unanimously on the president's authority to issue the order and the likelihood of success of the president on the merits of it, the Supreme Court said that the government's "interest in preserving national security is an urgent objective of the highest order."[606]

The Supreme Court's only change in the Trump travel pause was minimal: it did not overrule lower court injunctions to the extent they affected "foreign nationals who have a credible claim of a bona fide relationship with a person or entity in the United States," such as a family member or admission to a university. The Court's decision noted that even the Trump executive order had accounted for such situations "by establishing a case-by-case waiver system primarily for the benefit of individuals" with such ties to the United States.

FEDERAL COURT CHALLENGES TO THE TRAVEL PAUSE: THE NINTH CIRCUIT

Prior to the Supreme Court's decision upholding the president's authority and within days of the issuance of the president's first executive order, US District Judge James Robert in Seattle had enjoined it on the grounds that the order violated constitutional norms because, in his opinion, it was motivated by animus toward Islam.

So-called "Big Law" attorneys in private practice, with ties to the Obama administration, from firms like Jones Day, Arnold & Porter, and Akin Gump, quickly went to work preparing a mountain of briefs to support the ruling, which was appealed to the Ninth Circuit Court of Appeals.[607] Attorney Steve Berman filed a brief in support of the ruling on behalf of the Service Employees International Union, which had endorsed Hillary Clinton for president. Berman was quoted as saying "[p]ersonally I think that most people in my firm think the presidential order crossed the line and if we can help in that fight let's do it."[608]

The Ninth Circuit Court of Appeals, sitting in San Francisco, twice approved injunctions against Trump's orders, based on lower court rulings not just in Seattle but also Hawaii, in a lawsuit filed by a Honolulu-based Muslim cleric.[609]

THE FOURTH CIRCUIT

Responding to arguments that Trump had suggested he wanted to ban immigration by Muslims during his campaign, Jeffrey Wall, the Justice Department's Acting Solicitor General, explained to the Fourth US Circuit Court of Appeals, sitting in Richmond, Virginia, to hear a separate challenge to the order, "[t]his is not a Muslim ban," to conclude otherwise would require an "unprecedented kind of psychoanalysis" of Trump's alleged motives regarding an order that was facially neutral and well within the scope of presidential authority.[610]

Judge Paul Niemeyer, a Republican appointee, said that if the courts can examine Trump's statements as a presidential candidate to discern motives, "can we look at his college speeches? How about his speeches to businessmen 20 years ago?" An ACLU attorney pointed out at the Fourth Circuit hearing that more than 90 percent of the population of the six nations affected was Muslim and that judicial deference was not "a license to violate the establishment clause" requiring the government to remain neutral on religion.

On May 25, 2017, in a 10-3 decision that actually followed "party-line" appointments, the majority of Democrat-appointed Fourth Circuit judges ruled that Trump's executive order could not be enforced because it appeared to them to discriminate based on religion and that the administration's argument that the order was needed to protect national security was a "pretext" offered in "bad faith."[611] Trump's order "speaks with vague words of national security, but in context drips with religious intolerance, animus and discrimination," wrote Chief Judge Roger L. Gregory in an opinion that recited statements from candidate Trump during the campaign.

Judge Niemeyer, in dissent, derided the decision for ignoring rulings that called for deference to the president's authority over immigration and for "fabricating a new proposition of law" that allows judges to use campaign statements to decide on a president's actions in office. "The Supreme Court surely will shudder at the majority's adoption of this new rule that has no limits or bounds—one that transforms the majority's criticisms of a candidate's various campaign statements into a constitutional violation."

Niemeyer had accurately predicted the Supreme Court's reaction, which in large measure overturned the Fourth Circuit's and the Ninth Circuit's decisions upholding injunctions against the order.

California's Opposition to the Travel Pause

According to California Attorney General Xavier Becerra, "a number of attorneys general have been in conversations, *since before Trump even took office*, about doing everything possible to protect the rights of people" (emphasis added).[612] "In terms of the travel ban, it was a matter of trying to make sure we could make a good case that it was unconstitutional and it violated federal law," he added.[613]

Thus, attorneys general of fifteen states and the District of Columbia filed their own briefs in opposition to the travel pause (only two of the states represented were won by Trump),[614,615] and among them was Becerra, who said that Trump's order "threatens to rip apart California families, risks their economic well-being and defies centuries of America tradition."[616] After the Fourth Circuit issued its ruling upholding the injunctions on the travel pause, Becerra issued a statement saying:

[t]he Fourth Circuit has confirmed what we already know: Donald Trump's travel ban is anti-Muslim, un-American, and unconstitutional. We should protect our national security based on real threats, not on fear mongering and hate. We should continue to welcome people of all faiths and ethnicities to experience the greatness of America – to study at our universities, to contribute to cutting edge research, and to explore our national treasures. *This Administration already has suffered a string of well-deserved defeats in the courts. President Trump should read the Constitution. I will continue to fight discrimination and overreach every step of the way* [emphasis added].[617]

Becerra's statement was proven wrong, as Trump's "string of well-deserved defeats" ended in a unanimous Supreme Court victory. In responding to the

Supreme Court's decision upholding most of the travel pause, Becerra issued a statement attempting to spin the decision as a victory for his side because a part of the injunction was kept in place. The statement continued to erroneously refer to the order as a "Muslim travel ban" and repeated the wording of the "religious discrimination" justification for the overturned portion of the Fourth Circuit opinion, something the Supreme Court had definitely not agreed with.[618] Nevertheless, in late March 2017, the Public Policy Institute of California polled Californians and found that 58 percent disapproved of the temporary travel ban, whereas 37 percent approved.[619]

CALIFORNIA'S HYPOCRITICAL OWN TRAVEL BAN

While simultaneously arguing that Trump's travel ban should be blocked by federal courts on religious discrimination grounds, Becerra had no problem issuing his own extension of California's travel ban from four to eight states, based on his determination that they had enacted laws that are discriminatory toward sexual orientation and gender self-identification.[620] Many of the objectionable laws, however, were intended by the states to protect the same constitutionally protected religious rights that Becerra says Trump's travel pause offends.

According to the California ban and Becerra's determination, California now prohibits state-sanctioned travel to Texas, Alabama, Kentucky, South Dakota, Kansas, Mississippi, North Carolina, and Tennessee. The California law was first animated by a North Carolina proposal to overturn a city ordinance that allowed transgender people to use the public restroom of their choice rather than their birth gender. "There are consequences to discrimination," Becerra said, and "[r]estricting state-sponsored travel is a consequence."[621]

Becerra's idea of such discrimination includes laws in three of the states—Alabama, South Dakota, and Texas—intended to protect the religious-expression rights of faith-based adoption or foster agencies that refuse to place children with certain families, such as same-sex couples.[622]

Becerra's action extending the travel ban to Kentucky angered at least two mayors there who felt it was discriminatory. Openly gay Lexington Mayor Jim Gray, along with business and tourism leaders, wrote Becerra that their city had passed a "fairness" ordinance years ago; and Louisville Mayor Greg Fischer wrote that "inclusive" cities like his should be rewarded, not penalized.[623] Mayor Fischer claimed that Louisville had lost two conventions because of the ban.

Becerra refused to exempt Lexington from the ban on state-funded travel to Kentucky, stating that a law in Kentucky that "allows student-run organizations in schools to discriminate against classmates" runs afoul of the California ban and that Lexington would have to "make progress with leaders in your state to repeal or amend" the law, then California would remove Kentucky from the banned list.[624] Called "SB 17," the law is intended to protect religious expression in schools and give student religious organizations, in particular, more flexibility in choosing their own members.[625]

"California may be able to stop their state employees, but they can't stop all the businesses that are fleeing over taxation and regulation relocating to Texas," said a spokesman for the Texas governor on Becerra's decision to add Texas to the travel ban list.[626]

One of the states on Becerra's travel ban list is Alabama. Fresno State University, which has a college football program that is building national acclaim, is scheduled to play the mighty University of Alabama football team in Tuscaloosa next fall. A request for clarification on whether the state university's paid sports travel is exempt from the ban has been filed with Becerra, but no ruling has been issued.[627] Extending the law to the University of California at Berkeley and University of California at Los Angeles could have devastating effects on their top-tier college football programs, as many of the top teams in the nation with whom they compete, such as Texas, Texas A&M, TCU, Alabama, Auburn, and Tennessee, are located in states on Becerra's banned list.

The Wall and Immigration Policy

● ● ●

BETWEEN 2013 AND 2015, 2.1 million illegal entries into the United States were made across our nation's 1,900-mile southern border with Mexico, according to the Border Patrol.[628] From 2010 to 2015, existing fencing on the border, covering about 694 miles, was breached 9,200 times.[629] There are an estimated eleven million unauthorized immigrants living in the United States, and about 27 percent of them live in California;[630] other states with large populations of illegal immigrants include Texas, Florida, New York, New Jersey, and Illinois.[631] Fox News studied federal data and found that among those crossing the border illegally are a "widely disproportionate" number of hardcore criminals and that their toll of crime in the United States is significant, that they are three times as likely to be convicted of murder as members of the general population, and that crime in general caused by illegal immigrants is far more than their 3.5 percent share of the US population would suggest.[632] PolitiFact confirmed that a claim by Sean Hannity that illegal immigrants account for 75 percent of federal convictions for drug possession, as well as significant percentages of drug trafficking, kidnapping, murder, and other crimes identified by the US Sentencing Commission, was true.[633]

On the early evening of July 1, 2015, while taking a walk with her father in San Francisco at Pier 14 in the Embarcadero district, thirty-two-year-old Kate Steinle was shot in the back and killed by one of three bullets fired from a stolen gun by Juan Francisco Lopez-Sanchez, an illegal immigrant from Mexico who had been previously deported five times and who had been released from jail, with federal immigration charges pending, under San Francisco's "sanctuary-city" policies.[634]

Shortly after the Steinle murder, Donald Trump began speaking out about it. "This senseless and totally preventable act of violence committed by an illegal immigrant is yet another example of why we must secure our border immediately," said Trump in a statement on the tragedy two days later.[635] "This is an absolutely disgraceful situation and I am the only one who can fix it. Nobody else has the guts to even talk about it. That won't happen if I become President."[636] Trump went on to discuss the Steinle murder many times on the campaign trail as an example of why illegal immigration should be stemmed, and he brought up the murder in his speech to the Republican National Convention in Cleveland.[637]

Yet, Trump had the idea to build a formidable southern-border barrier early in his campaign for the presidency and before the tragedy in San Francisco. In his announcement for the presidency on June 16, 2015, Trump said, "I will build a great wall—and nobody builds walls better than me, believe me—and I'll build them very inexpensively. I will build a great, great wall on our southern border, and I will make Mexico pay for that wall. Mark my words."[638] During his campaign, Trump issued a vision on immigration policy to promote legal immigration, to keep immigration levels within historical norms, and to establish new immigration controls to boost wages and jobs "offered to American workers first." Among a "Ten-Point" policy plan including ending "catch-and-release," ending sanctuary cities, and ensuring that a biometric entry–exit visa-tracking system is fully implemented, Trump's first stated policy point was to begin working "on an impenetrable physical wall on the southern border."[639]

Mexican leaders' reaction to the idea of their country paying for the wall was predictably negative.[640] Nevertheless, President Trump made good on his campaign pledge by requesting that Congress allocate the necessary funds to undertake construction, with the intention that Mexico will pay for the wall…eventually.[641]

"I couldn't be more disappointed that President Trump has used his first budget proposal to prioritize the border wall—his pet project—and a deportation force over critical support for state and local law enforcement," said US Senator Dianne Feinstein in reaction to Trump's commitment in his first budget proposal to fulfill his campaign promise.[642] Yet, according to

Sacramento Bee columnist Dan Walters, it was Feinstein herself twenty-three years ago, when running in a tight race for her Senate seat, who declared in an ad that she "led the fight to stop illegal immigration," noting the need for more border guards, lighting, and fencing.[643]

San Diego is a "high-priority" area for building the border wall, according to documents obtained from the Department of Homeland Security by the *San Diego Union-Tribune*.[644] Contracts for prototypes for the wall were scheduled to be awarded in June of 2017, with construction to be under way midsummer and $20 million already committed for the creation, construction, and establishment of wall design standards and other types of barriers.[645] About 460 companies replied to requests for proposals to build the wall. The Trump administration's instructions for winning bids for the wall said they must have a design that is thirty feet tall, can't be climbed, and is constructed in a way to prevent digging from below for at least six feet, with the side facing the United States "aesthetically pleasing in color."[646]

In April 2017, US Attorney General Jeff Sessions visited the southwestern border at Nogales, Arizona, and San Diego County and referred to these areas as "ground zero" in the fight against "transnational gangs like MS-13 and international cartels that flood our country with drugs and leave death and violence in their wake."[647] Sessions's visit surely highlighted that President Trump was going to keep his promises on stronger border and immigration control.

At the border in Nogales, Sessions announced a new policy that each of the ninety-four US attorney's offices must designate one of its prosecutors as a border security coordinator, among other program changes intended to strengthen charging and prosecution of repeat offenders and those aiding them.[648] Sessions said, "for those that continue to seek improper and illegal entry into this country, be forewarned: this is a new era. This is the Trump era. The lawlessness, the abdication of the duty to enforce our immigration laws, and the catch and release practices are over."[649] Sessions further announced measures to accelerate processing of immigration cases and a plan to add 125 more immigration judges to the existing 301 to work out the incredible backlog of 540,000 immigration cases built up during the Obama era.

While at the San Diego border, Sessions made an explicit reference to the nearby city of Escondido, saying that the city is in the midst of an increase in street-gang violence inspired by Mexican gangs, involving increased crime, "more shootings, more guns, more neighborhoods terrorized."[650] Sessions's visit to the California border drew criticism rather than support from California State Attorney General Xavier Becerra, calling the federal immigration crackdown "reckless."[651]

Sessions responded on ABC's *This Week* by saying that state and local governments cannot by federal law prohibit their law-enforcement officers from sharing information with the federal government. Sessions said:

> In other words, if a person commits a crime in Los Angeles or in the case of Kate Steinle, San Francisco, and an individual there is released multiple times and he comes back to San Francisco because it's a sanctuary city and commits a murder, that's the kind of situation that that person should have been deported previously and not allowed to return.[652]

Even before initiation of construction of the wall, Trump's promise to strictly enforce current immigration law has seen dramatic results. Border apprehensions of illegals attempting to enter the United States from Mexico hit a seventeen-year low in March 2017 of 12,500 people.[653]

Compared with the same period just one year before, apprehensions were down 61 percent,[654] and the number of parents with children was down 93 percent from the previous December.[655] Although illegal border crossings diminished in the early days of the Trump administration, arrests of criminal illegal immigrants increased by 33 percent over the prior year's comparable time period under Obama, from 16,104 to 21,262.[656]

ILLEGAL ALIENS AND CRIME

The Steinle murder in San Francisco is, sadly, not the only crime of a criminal illegal alien in California to reach the headlines. Constantino Banda-Acosta, who was in the state illegally and had been deported fifteen times, was speeding, ran a stop sign, and committed a hit-and-run after severely injuring a six-year-old boy in San Ysidro near the border. The young boy was in another car just a block away from home after a family trip to Disneyland. Banda-Acosta, who has a criminal history that includes domestic violence, was suspected of drunk driving.[657]

A Department of Homeland Security report found that from 2011 to 2013, about 1.9 million legal and illegal immigrants had committed crimes that qualified for deportation proceedings. In 2015, the Migration Policy Institute, a nonpartisan think tank, estimated that roughly 820,000 illegal immigrants have serious criminal records.[658]

The FBI and federal immigration agents have come to routinely and periodically, even under the Obama administration, conduct surprise raids to capture evidence and criminal illegals in California. In May 2017, 188 people were arrested in a five-day sweep across Southern California targeting public-safety threats that netted 169 foreign nationals with prior criminal convictions, including fifteen people convicted of sex crimes, a convicted rapist, a previously deported cocaine trafficker, and two people convicted of cruelty to a child.[659]

In April 2017, agents searched a hotel and two homes in San Gabriel and Arcadia in Los Angeles County for evidence in an alleged $50 million visa-fraud scheme that gave US permanent resident cards to Chinese nationals, including criminals on China's most-wanted list.[660] By this example, clearly, the criminal immigration problem in California is not limited to issues just at the southern border.

Over one hundred Chinese nationals who wanted so-called "green cards" were lured to invest in a fraudulent program that allows foreigners to get the card through an "EB-5 visa program" by investing at least $500,000 in an American business that creates ten new jobs. However, the funds were diverted to personal uses, illegally, by the organizers of the fund.[661]

CALIFORNIA OPPOSITION TO "THE WALL" AND IMMIGRATION REFORMS
An article published in *Salon* summed up the collision course between California's political leaders and the Trump administration on immigration policy:

[I]n states like California, where one in three residents is foreign born and half the children have at least one immigrant parent, state and local governments are moving to thwart any massive new deportation effort. From the highest political circles in the legislature, to briefings by county agencies telling employees not to assist federal immigration police, to local cities declaring themselves sanctuaries, a colossal struggle is taking shape.[662]

Some of California's liberal leaders' reactions to Trump's election and to the prospect of the wall actually being built have been nearly hysterical, sadly predictable, yet still breathtaking. In April 2017, State Senator Ricardo Lara, D-Bell Gardens, introduced legislation to prohibit the state from contracting with any person or organization that provides any goods or services for the wall, "to say that building a wasteful and unnecessary wall would be a huge mistake."[663] Lara wanted Californians to vote on the wall as well, but that version of his bill has been slowed down, likely because it would be unconstitutional. San Francisco supervisors introduced legislation to prevent the city from contracting with companies that placed bids on constructing the wall, regardless of whether they actually win the bids.[664]

The Berkeley City Council passed a unanimous resolution recommending the city divest funds from any company involved in any aspect of the wall project, and the Oakland City Council also voted to bar that city from entering into contracts with any companies that work on the wall.[665] A Los Angeles councilman introduced a motion that would require companies seeking contracts with the city to disclose publicly in advance whether they have submitted bids to build the wall.[666] And other members of the state legislature introduced legislation that would require state pension funds to divest in companies that win contracts to build the wall.[667]

Political grandstanding against the border wall isn't limited in Los Angeles to just city council members—it includes a delegation of Mexican governors from Baja California, Sonora, Morelos, Durango, Guanajuato, and Oaxaca. Speaking at a ceremonial exchange at Los Angeles City Hall, the Baja California governor said, "[w]alls are very complicated...they are offensive."[668]

Governor Brown's response to the wall has been more measured. During an interview on NBC's *Meet the Press*, Brown said California "will fight very hard" against the wall, but will not bring "stupid lawsuits" against it; rather, "we'll be strategic."[669] Brown added, "we're not here to protect criminals. But we do recognize that America's the land of opportunity. All of our parents came here at one time, our grandparents, our great-grandparents, they came here. That's what builds the state."

Nevertheless, lawsuits have been filed to stall Trump's wall in California. The Center for Biological Diversity, an environmental group, filed a legal challenge against the Trump administration to halt the proposed prototype versions of the wall that are intended to be built first in San Diego County.[670] Although funding for an overall border wall will require congressional action, funding is available for an initial stretch to test ideas in the Otay Mesa area of San Diego County. In San Diego County, the border with Mexico is sixty miles long, but not all of it has physical barriers in place.[671]

The wall and the prospect of deportations of criminal aliens have engendered a "fear of mass deportations" that has been fodder for political theater across the state. Los Angeles Mayor Eric Garcetti and Los Angeles County Supervisor Hilda Solis, both Democrats, announced a $10 million fund to hire lawyers "to defend local immigrants without legal status" even before Trump was inaugurated.[672] Governor Brown's 2018 budget proposal included an additional $15 million, according to the *Los Angeles Times*, to "help *Californians* facing deportation" (emphasis added).[673] Presumably, Californians are also US citizens who would not face deportation, but the distinction was apparently lost on the headline writer for the newspaper.

In late March 2017, the Trump administration released the first ever report on law-enforcement agencies that are potentially endangering the public by failing to cooperate with ICE agents seeking detainers of criminal illegal aliens, naming multiple jurisdictions in California. Of local jurisdictions nationwide cited as failing to honor ICE immigration detainers and release serious criminals to federal authorities, in the reporting period, the Los Angeles Police Department and the Los Angeles County Sheriff's Department were revealed to have declined federal detainers for five people with criminal convictions. Four of the individuals were Mexican citizens, and one was a Salvadoran. One of the suspects was convicted of arson, two of domestic violence, and two of assault. Other California locations where federal detainer requests were not honored included the Alameda County Jail, Madera County Jail, Anaheim City Jail, and the Sacramento, Santa Barbara, and Santa Clara County Jails.[674] According to a report disseminated by the Center for Immigration Studies, Santa Clara County, in Silicon Valley, led the nation for denied detention requests for aliens for the period January 1, 2014, through September 30, 2015, with a stunning 1,856 total denied detainers for the period, and 964 of those were for individuals having prior criminal records. The next highest county was Los Angeles, with 1,492 declined detainers, including 1,290 for individuals with prior criminal records.[675]

Silicon Valley's "H-1B" Visa Concerns

In April 2017 the US Justice Department warned companies against favoring foreign, temporary-visa workers in hiring, firing, or recruiting efforts.[676] The warning came as the Trump administration issued an executive order to address fraud and abuse in the program and began a review of reportedly hundreds of thousands of applications for so-called "H-1B visas," which is a type of visa granted to persons who have highly specialized skills.[677] Immigration attorneys have said the changes could particularly affect California-based Silicon Valley firms, which seek foreign workers arguably at the expense of recruiting domestic workers. One news report about an outsourcing controversy involving the visas alleged that 250 computer programmers were laid off at Walt Disney World and wrongfully replaced by foreign workers with the H-1B visa.[678] Roughly 236,000 applications were received for foreign workers in 2016 by the US Citizenship and Immigration Services (USCIS), but only 85,000 visas were granted.[679]

One news report alleged that foreign employees' salaries are higher than standard wages in the technology industry.[680] Yet the same report included an observation by an immigration attorney that the system is not perfect and that "[o]ne of the complaints is that [certain] companies try to game the system, and are driving the salary to the lowest level every time."[681] Added a fellow at the Center for Immigration Studies, the "program is a mess, it is a simple thing. You shouldn't be able to replace an American with an H-1B worker under any circumstances."[682]

In 2017, for the first time in years, the number of H-1B visa applications decreased. Experts reportedly said the decrease was a signal that Trump's "America First" rhetoric alone is deterring employers from hiring foreign workers under the program. The USCIS reported that it had received 199,000 applications for the next fiscal year, down from the 236,000 in 2016 and below the 233,000 it received in 2015.[683]

ILLEGAL IMMIGRANTS AND CALIFORNIA'S ACCOMMODATING GOVERNMENT

California now issues driver's licenses to illegal immigrants. In fact, during 2015 alone, 52 percent, or 397,000 out of 759,000 total licenses issued, went to illegals.[684] In October 2013, Governor Brown signed the legislation offering illegal immigrants the right to have identity documentation and drive in California.[685] In effect, Brown authorized providing official legal documents to those in the state illegally, people who do not even qualify for Social Security numbers because they are not legal citizens. Two years after the implementation of AB 60,[686] the Motor Voter Act, an estimated 806,000 illegal aliens have received California driver's licenses, according to Department of Motor Vehicles (DMV) statistics.[687]

California's driver's licenses for illegal immigrants have raised serious national security concerns, as have the designs for such licenses in other states. Under federal law, states can issue driving privilege documentation to illegals, but the licenses are not valid for federal purposes, such as identification to board an airliner. California's original plan was to make the licenses for illegals look exactly the same as those for citizens. The Department of Homeland Security objected, and design changes were mandated to alert to the fact that the cards could not be used for federal identification purposes.[688]

Ironically, many of the illegal aliens who received driver's licenses under AB 60 now fear federal immigration authorities will access their Department of Motor Vehicles information in order to initiate deportation under President Trump. But not without a fight from the states' top Democrats. "We're consulting with our lawyers to make sure [data] is not accessible to federal authorities for any deportation proceedings," Senate President Pro Tempore Kevin de León, D-Los Angeles, warned.[689] Assembly Speaker Anthony Rendon, D-Paramount, said, "and if you want to get to them, you have to go through us."[690]

Under AB 60, the DMV was to maintain a separate database of the specialty license holders. However, late in 2016, a DMV informant said that the DMV not only instructed programmers to immediately remove AB 60 administrative coding, but the agency now claims it does not maintain a separate database of AB 60 license holders.[691] "Databases available to law enforcement entities do not indicate whether a driver license was issued under AB 60, nor do they include any of the identification documents used to obtain a driver license, AB 60 or otherwise," a recent DMV statement said.[692]

WELFARE BENEFITS AND STATE SUBSIDIES FOR ILLEGAL ALIENS

Adult illegal aliens also may receive free health care from Medi-Cal and join California's form of Obamacare subsidized insurance, "Covered California." SB 4,[693] authored by State Senator Ricardo Lara, D-Los Angeles, passed in 2015 and was signed into law by Brown. SB 4 extended health-care coverage to low-income undocumented immigrant children, with the end goal of providing coverage for all undocumented immigrants, according to Lara.[694]

Lara is also the author of the Health for All Act, SB 1005,[695] which is a single-payer, state-government-run health system. Lara claims his plan "will expand health insurance coverage to individuals who are currently excluded through Medi-Cal if individuals meet income requirements, or through an exchange program where they can purchase private health insurance."[696] This legislation specifically includes and insures illegal aliens.

Medi-Cal is California's version of the national welfare program for free medical care for the poor known as Medicaid. According to the state Department of Health Care Services website, "[y]ou do not have to be a citizen or have satisfactory immigration status to qualify for Medi-Cal."[697] Children of illegal aliens born in the United States qualify for Medi-Cal free health insurance as well.

In addition, whether a member of Medi-Cal or not, although federal law generally bars illegal immigrants from being covered by Medicaid, a little-known part of the state–federal health insurance program for the poor pays about $2 billion a year for emergency treatment for a group of patients who, according to hospitals, mostly comprise illegal immigrants. Most of it goes to reimburse hospitals for delivering babies for women who show up in their emergency rooms, according to interviews with hospital officials and studies described by PBS.[698] The California Department of Health Care Services says, "[a]n immigrant who meets all eligibility requirements, but is not in a satisfactory immigration status for full scope Medi-Cal is entitled to emergency and pregnancy-related services and, when needed, state-funded long-term care."[699]

Illegal aliens may also receive welfare benefits. Although federally supported the Supplemental Nutrition Assistance Program (SNAP; "food stamps") benefits of about $125 per person are technically not available to illegal immigrants, in California "CalFresh" offices, illegal immigrants are not discouraged from applying for the program. According to CalFresh, "Being a CalFresh beneficiary will not affect an applicant's immigration status or the immigration status of their family. A petitioner may apply for food stamps for their family without applying for themselves. The Department of Social Services will not share any applicant information with the United States Citizenship and Immigration Services (USCIS). This includes information needed to ascertain the eligibility and benefits for other members of the household. Immigration officials could not use this information to deport someone unless there is a criminal violation involved."[700]

Illegal alien college students may receive Cal-Grants and state-funded college scholarships, as well as lower in-state tuition rates. In August 2015, Brown signed legislation striking the word "alien" from the state's labor code, as well as a measure to even allow illegal aliens to serve as election poll workers.[701]

The Toll of Illegal Immigration on Californians

California's accommodation of illegal immigration surely comes with a cost to society. According to one report, illegal immigrants cost California $30.29 billion a year,[702] close to 17 percent of Brown's 2018 state budget. Another report by the Federation for Immigration Reform pegs the cost to California taxpayers at $25 billion annually.[703] Using either figure, there is no doubt that illegal immigration greatly strains the California social net. As political consultant Mike Madrid told the *Los Angeles Times*, "[w]e've passed the Rubicon here...This is not an academic debate on the U.S. Senate floor about legal and illegal and how you want to build the wall...the state doesn't have the luxury of being ideological...The undocumented are not going anywhere."[704]

In just Los Angeles County, the cost is tremendous, according to former county supervisor Mike Antonovich. "Illegal immigration continues to cost Los Angeles County taxpayers alone nearly $2 billion a year, and siphons resources away from vital municipal services for legal immigrants and county residents," wrote Antonovich in 2014.[705] According to Antonovich, 25 percent of county jail inmates are illegals, costing the county $550 million annually. In addition to these costs are, according to Antonovich, "no-cost, cradle-to-grave federal and state benefits for illegals and reimbursement for costs incurred by local governments"; Antonovich added that "effective immigration reform must include a comprehensive approach to fix our broken system."

There is no question that President Trump has announced new policies to attempt to "fix our broken system." It remains an open question, however, whether California officials will let the broken system be fixed.

Rising Crime In California

● ● ●

AFTER A DECADES-LONG DECLINE IN violent and property crime, crime is once again on the rise in the Golden State, and it is self-induced.[706] President Trump has vowed to reduce violent crime across the country and in the most violent cities.[707]

California's self-induced crime spike is at least in part a result of Governor Jerry Brown's "prison realignment" legislation, AB 109,[708] which shifted responsibility for thirty thousand criminal offenders from the state to the counties. Whereas state prisons have been relieved of their prison population, lesser county jails have become flooded with offenders, many of them responsible for more serious criminal charges than those usually seen in the permanent populations of the county jail system. The system has become ripe for early releases because of crowding, without much concern for recidivism rates.

Brown also backed, in 2014, a measure titled Proposition 47, and in 2016 another measure, Proposition 57, which let so-called "low-level" convicts out of county jails, while "low-level, nonviolent" state prisoners were dropped down into county jails.[709,710] Propositions 47 and 57 also reclassified felons with prior convictions for armed robbery, kidnapping, carjacking, child abuse, residential burglary, arson, assault with a deadly weapon, and many other crimes. That reclassification ultimately eliminates jail time for some serious offenders.[711] For example, under the reforms, a person arrested in California who illegally possesses a stolen gun will be prosecuted not for a felony, as in the past, but rather a misdemeanor, if the value of the weapon is less than $950.

Although liberals will object to the connection between these reforms and crime rates, consequently, crime in California is on an upward trajectory.[712] Californians are seeing more incidences of armed robbery, kidnapping, carjacking, child abuse, residential burglary, arson, and assault with a deadly weapon, and it will get worse, according to law-enforcement professionals throughout the state.[713]

As stated, prior to passage of Proposition 47, many crimes classified as "arrestable" as a felony are now only "citable" as a misdemeanor. That means offenders may not be booked into jail but instead given a citation, like a traffic ticket, with a court date to appear, and then released.[714] Law enforcement officials report that the courts no longer have the authority or the teeth to enforce court appearances, and these criminals walk freely.[715]

Officer Keith Boyer of the Whittier Police Department was murdered, and his partner Officer Patrick Hazell was wounded, in a shootout in February 2017 by Michael Mejia, who was driving a stolen car. Mejia murdered the car's owner prior to stealing it. Mejia had been arrested five times in the past seven months while under the supervision of Orange County authorities as part of AB 109.[716]

The California Department of Corrections and Rehabilitation reports that 75 percent of recidivists commit their reentry crime within a year of release.[717] With AB 109, Proposition 47 and Proposition 57 statistics potentially exploding with recidivist offenders, the Democrats in the legislature passed AB 1050, ordering the Board of State and Community Corrections to redefine "recidivism" in an obvious effort to manipulate recidivism statistics.[718]

"The most recent statistics from the U.S. Department of Justice show violent crime rates in some California cities has increased by over 50 percent," said Michele Hanisee, president of the Association of Los Angeles Deputy District Attorneys. "If you look at the nation data, our violent crime rates are going up faster than the rest of the nation."[719]

Violent crime is indeed on the rise in Los Angeles for the third straight year, which local officials attribute in part to increased gang violence.[720] "Rampant looting of cars" parked on the streets of San Francisco is up 31 percent, at nearly triple the crime rates in the last five years.[721] More than seventy cars are broken into daily in San Francisco, totaling 25,899 reported property crimes in 2015, and that number is growing.[722]

Recently, roving bands of criminal youths and likely gang members have been terrorizing passengers on the Bay Area Rapid Transit System (BART), and their strong-arm kicking and punching attacks have even been witnessed by a local mayor, who took pictures of their victims.[723] In one incident, an estimated forty to sixty "kids" boarded a train in crime-ridden Oakland and robbed seven passengers, beating up two of them.[724] Oakland is considered as one of the top-ten most dangerous cities in the United States, according to FBI statistics and *Forbes* magazine.[725] Several other BART robbery and mayhem incidents have occurred, and BART has surveillance video of the crimes, but regardless of a sense of justice for the victims, and in typical Bay Area liberal fashion, BART refuses to release videos of the surveillance because it "would create a high level of racially insensitive commentary toward the district."[726]

The *Sacramento Bee*'s Dan Walters reported a "sharp increase in crime" throughout California, citing an FBI state-by-state breakdown revealing a 7.6 percent increase in violent crime in California, well above the 3 percent increase nationally for the year.[727] The homicide rate in California well exceeds national averages.[728] Even nonpartisan organizations such as PolitiFact California[729] and CALMatters,[730] have conceded that the most recent statistics show that violent crime is on the rise in the state.

WHAT CAN BE DONE?

Clearly, federal and state cooperation in attacking gang violence in California could make a difference. According to a detailed article in *City Journal*, some of the most violent criminals at large in Los Angeles today are illegal aliens.[731]

President Trump signed three executive orders in February 2017 to crack down on violence in America.[732] The orders direct the US Department of Justice to form a task force and take necessary steps to specifically target criminal gangs and reduce violent crime and crime against police.[733]

In April, nine jurisdictions were notified by the Justice Department that they stand to lose federal law enforcement funding unless they cooperate.[734] The administration sent letters to officials in California, New York, Chicago, Philadelphia, and New Orleans—all places the Justice Department's inspector general identified as limiting the information local law enforcement can provide to federal immigration authorities about those in their custody.[735]

"And just several weeks ago in California's Bay Area, after a raid captured 11 MS-13 members on charges including murder, extortion and drug trafficking, city officials seemed more concerned with reassuring illegal immigrants that the raid was unrelated to immigration than with warning other MS-13 members that they were next," the DOJ notices said.[736] "The letters remind the recipient jurisdictions that, as a condition for receiving certain financial year 2016 funding from the Department of Justice, each of these jurisdictions agreed to provide documentation and an opinion from legal counsel validating that they are in compliance."[737]

Homeland Security Secretary John Kelly threatened additional consequences for local police departments that don't comply with federal authorities and deliver those criminal illegal aliens in custody, saying the alternative is immigration agents searching neighborhoods, known more commonly as immigration sweeps.[738]

> "Ideally the best place for us to pick up these illegal criminals is in jails and prisons," Kelly said at a news conference with AG Jeff Sessions in San Diego, next to a border fence topped with razor wire. "If they don't do that, then we have to go into neighborhoods. We have to go into courthouses. We have to go wherever we can find them and apprehend them."[739]

In a desperate reply, California's Senate President Kevin de León defiantly said the Trump administration's policies are based on "principles of white supremacy" and not American values.[740] Yet a 2011 Government Accountability Office report revealed that the typical criminal alien inmate in federal prisons has been arrested twelve times.[741] The arrest data for the criminal aliens in state and federal jails found that they were arrested for a total of about 2.9 million offenses, averaging about twelve each.[742]

Using recent statistics from Los Angeles, another sanctuary city, "Los Angeles saw all crime rise in 2015: violent crime up 19.9 percent, homicides up 10.2 percent, shooting victims up 12.6 percent, rapes up 8.6 percent, robberies up 12.3 percent, and aggravated assault up 27.5 percent...[sanctuary cities] encourage further illegal immigration and promote an underground economy that sabotages the tax base," the Daily Wire reported in 2016.[743] As Ian Smith pointed out in a *National Review* column in 2015:[744]

> It is estimated that fully half of America's 41 million immigrants have settled in just five metropolitan areas: New York City–Newark, Los Angeles, Chicago, Miami, and San Francisco–Oakland. According to data from the Center for Immigration Studies, every one of these cities and their surrounding counties has sanctuary policies of some kind. Considering the illegal-alien pull factor of these policies, which Kate Steinle's murderer admitted to, it's unsurprising that the immigrant populations of these sanctuary cities includes many who are here illegally.

The data and facts are staggering and clearly have nothing to do with "principles of white supremacy."[745]

California's liberal leaders have made grave mistakes about prison overcrowding and sentencing reduction that can be directly linked to the current rise in violent crime in the state. Rather than deny the data, these leaders ought to understand that their political correctness, as typified in the refusal of BART officials to release surveillance videos of crimes, does not serve either public safety or justice; rather, it protects the criminals, just as sanctuary-city policies have dumped hundreds of criminal offenders back onto the streets in disrespect of federal law. California needs an attitude adjustment on how it treats criminal offenders, and failure to do so will only point in the direction of less respect for the law and more crime, no matter what the federal government and Donald Trump's administration do to help solve the problem.

ACKNOWLEDGMENTS

● ● ●

CALIFORNIA'S WAR AGAINST DONALD TRUMP was an opportunity for two authors who love to write about politics—Katy Grimes and Jim Lacy—to establish a collaboration, and it was a rewarding partnership not just because of the depth of the material but also because both of us worked very well together from start to finish. We both are thankful for the opportunity to bring our ideas together in this work, and we especially thank our respective spouses, Terry and Janice, for their stellar support.

We received excellent editorial assistance from John Hrabe, and we so appreciate the help of Darin Henry, who was able to make our ideas on designing the cover of the book work. The line editing of this book by CreateSpace at Amazon was top-notch.

However, we want to offer a special acknowledgment to all those countless Californians who understand the many serious problems of our great state—and the need for reform—and who love the state as much as we do, with never a thought of leaving. If there is ever to be change in this beautiful place, it will be because you stayed, paid the taxes, spoke up, and made a difference.

ABOUT THE AUTHORS

● ● ●

JAMES V. LACY IS A frequent guest on the Fox Business News Channel's *Varney & Company* and appears on CNN/CNNi, France 24, and the Australian Broadcasting Corporation. He is the author of the Politico.com best seller *Taxifornia: Liberals' Laboratory to Bankrupt America* and author/editor of *Taxifornia 2016*. Lacy, a skilled election lawyer, served as a general counsel in the Reagan administration. He was a delegate for Reagan in 1976 and Donald Trump in 2016 to the Republican National Convention. He lives in Dana Point, California, with his wife, Janice. Lacy is the publisher of the California Political Review at www.capoliticalreview.com.

KATY GRIMES is a longtime investigative political journalist and analyst and has been an influential political blogger since 2004. Katy reports on the California Legislature and politics from the State Capitol for the Flash Report, Canada Free Press, and Reagan Babe, and she contributes to Legal Insurrection, World Net Daily, and Frontpage Mag. Katy is a frequent guest on many talk-radio shows and has worked for the Sacramento Union and the Pacific Research Institute's CalWatchdog Journalism Center. Katy was a contributor to James Lacy's *Taxifornia 2016*. A California native, Katy lives in Sacramento with her husband, Terry.

CHAPTER NOTES

INTRODUCTION

1. https://www.washingtonpost.com/lifestyle/style/this-is-california-in-the-era-of-trump/2017/03/22/04e349e2-02b0-11e7-b1e9-a05d3c21f7cf_story.html?utm_term=.33673306d8df

2. Ibid

3. http://www.sacbee.com/news/politics-government/politics-columns-blogs/dan-walters/article133751609.html

4. http://www.sacbee.com/news/politics-government/politics-columns-blogs/dan-walters/article37733694.html

5. Ibid

6. http://chiefexecutive.net/2017-best-worst-states-business/

CHAPTER 1: THE PLAYERS

7. http://www.PolitiFact.com/truth-o-meter/statements/2016/dec/04/mike-pence/mike-pence-says-donald-trump-won-most-counties-rep/

8. https://www.nytimes.com/2016/11/09/us/politics/hillary-clinton-donald-trump-president.html?mcubz=3

9. http://www.investors.com/politics/commentary/its-official-clintons-popular-vote-win-came-entirely-from-california/

10. http://www.investors.com/politics/commentary/its-official-clintons-popular-vote-win-came-entirely-from-california/

11. https://townhall.com/tipsheet/mattvespa/2016/12/17/without-california-trump-would-won-14-million-more-votes-than-clinton-n2261014

12. http://abcnews.go.com/Politics/OTUS/obama-romney-stand-big-issues/story?id=17611080

13. http://www.PolitiFact.com/truth-o-meter/article/2016/jul/15/donald-trumps-top-10-campaign-promises/

14. http://www.cbsnews.com/news/2016-election-donald-trump-hillary-clinton-climate-change/

15. https://www.donaldjtrump.com/100/

16. https://www.wsj.com/articles/trumps-deregulation-project-1492470927

17. https://www.donaldjtrump.com/100/

18. https://www.donaldjtrump.com/100/

19. http://time.com/4748860/trump-100-days-achievements/

20. http://wvmetronews.com/2017/06/05/president-trump-fulfills-campaign-promises-for-west-virginia/

21. http://www.latimes.com/politics/essential/la-pol-ca-essential-politics-updates-we-re-ready-to-fight-says-gov-jerry-1481739836-htmlstory.html

22. http://legalinsurrection.com/2017/01/cas-democratic-politicians-cover-themselves-in-trump-hate-social-justice-shame/

23. http://www.sfchronicle.com/politics/article/Anti-Trump-movement-nears-100th-day-of-resistance-11101666.php

24. https://www.gov.ca.gov/news.php?id=19669

25. http://www.nbcnews.com/meet-the-press/video/full-brown-interview-you-don-t-want-to-mess-with-california-905023555599

26. Ibid

27. http://www.mercurynews.com/2017/02/11/gov-jerry-brown-asks-potential-nemesis-president-trump-for-aid/

28. http://www.californiamuseum.org/inductee/edmund-g-pat-brown

29. http://patbrowndocumentary.com/synopsis/

30. Ibid

31. https://www.forbes.com/sites/joelkotkin/2011/01/03/californias-third-brown-era/2/#5eee29cd3b5e

32. https://www.californiataxdata.com/pdf/Prop13.pdf

33. http://www.ocregister.com/2016/10/28/when-voters-cleaned-house-at-the-state-supreme-court/

34. http://www.scpr.org/news/2010/03/08/12671/jerry-brown-talks-about-buddhism-and-governing/

35. Ibid

36. Ibid

37. http://www.wtp.org/

38. https://www.law.berkeley.edu/files/Crime_Trends_in_the_City_of_Oakland_-_A_25-Year_Look.pdf

39. https://www.usatoday.com/story/money/business/2016/10/01/most-dangerous-cities-america/91227778/

40. https://www.law.berkeley.edu/files/Crime_Trends_in_the_City_of_Oakland_-_A_25-Year_Look.pdf

41. http://www.mcclatchydc.com/news/politics-government/article24540676.html

42. https://cei.org/sites/default/files/Hans%20Bader%20-%20The%20Nation's%20Worst%20State%20Attorneys%20General_1.pdf

43. Ibid

44. http://ww2.kqed.org/news/2015/01/05/an-annotated-guide-to-jerry-browns-state-of-the-state-address/

45. http://time.com/4645830/california-jerry-brown-donald-trump-speech-transcript/

46. Ibid

47. http://www.sactax.org/2017/01/jerry-browns-big-green-budget-is-in-the-red/

48. Ibid

49. http://californiapolicycenter.org/california-high-speed-rails-dubious-claims-of-environmental-benefits/

50. http://www.latimes.com/local/political/la-me-pc-mccarthy-high-speed-rail-20140613-story.html

51. http://www.mercurynews.com/2017/02/07/editorial-is-kevin-mccarthy-sabotaging-caltrain-electrification/

52. http://www.nationalreview.com/article/390562/kim-jong-un-style-coronation-california-democrat-tim-cavanaugh
http://www.dailynews.com/government-and-politics/20140616/senate-elects-los-angeles-democrat-kevin-de-leon-as-next-leader

53. http://www.laweekly.com/news/kevin-de-leon-went-from-college-dropout-to-californias-senate-president-8175519

54. http://www.breitbart.com/california/2017/02/05/california-state-senate-leader-family-illegal-false-documents-deportation/

55. Ibid

56. http://leginfo.legislature.ca.gov/faces/billNavClient.xhtml?bill_id=201520160SB350

57. https://ww2.kqed.org/news/2016/08/23/tougher-greenhouse-gas-emission-limits-move-forward-in-legislature/

58. Ibid

59. http://www.latimes.com/politics/essential/la-pol-ca-essential-politics-updates-california-senate-leader-says-white-1492803106-htmlstory.html

60. http://www.sandiegouniontribune.com/business/economy/sd-fi-sb30-trump-20170406-story.html

61. http://www.sacbee.com/news/politics-government/capitol-alert/article141092843.html

62. http://www.sfchronicle.com/opinion/diaz/article/State-attorney-general-leader-of-the-California-11243773.php

63. https://www.gov.ca.gov/news.php?id=19614

64. Ibid

65. http://www.latimes.com/politics/essential/la-pol-ca-essential-politics-updates-gov-brown-taps-california-s-rep-1480609606-htmlstory.html

66. Ibid

67. http://www.trevorloudon.com/2013/01/marxist-labor-leaders-used-latino-voters-to-move-california-left-implications-for-the-entire-us/

68. http://www.breitbart.com/california/2017/01/11/california-declare-legal-war-trump-administration/

69. http://www.sacbee.com/news/politics-government/capitol-alert/article150294732.html

70. http://www.frontpagemag.com/fpm/265032/brown-becerra-axis-illegals-lloyd-billingsley

71. http://www.sacbee.com/news/politics-government/capitol-alert/article129457614.html

72. https://oag.ca.gov/news/press-releases/attorney-general-xavier-becerra-issues-statement-trump-administrations-executive

73.   https://www.usnews.com/news/best-states/california/articles/2017-05-04/california-attorney-general-wants-more-money-to-fight-trump

74.   http://www.mercurynews.com/2017/05/11/jerry-brown-unveils-new-state-budget-proposal-thursday/

75.   http://abcnews.go.com/ThisWeek/video/ca-attorney-general-mexico-taxpayers-pay-medieval-wall-46968238

76.   Ibid

77.   https://www.feinstein.senate.gov/public/index.cfm/biography

78.   http://www.notablebiographies.com/Du-Fi/Feinstein-Dianne.html

79.   http://www.washingtontimes.com/news/2009/apr/21/senate-husbands-firm-cashes-in-on-crisis/

80.   http://www.washingtontimes.com/news/2013/jun/12/firm-chaired-by-sen-feinsteins-husband-cashes-in-o/

81.   http://www.breitbart.com/big-government/2015/01/17/sen-feinsteins-husbands-company-to-bag-1-billion-for-government-deal/

82.   Ibid

83.   http://losangeles.cbslocal.com/2017/04/20/sen-feinstein-holds-heated-town-hall-in-south-la/

84.   http://www.politico.com/story/2017/05/21/feinstein-scalded-by-anti-trump-fervor-238641

85. http://www.sfchronicle.com/news/article/Feinstein-Harris-will-have-some-pull-on-federal-10828126.php#comments

86. Ibid

87. http://www.capoliticalreview.com/top-stories/feinstein-continues-to-block-necessary-water-project/

88. http://www.sacbee.com/news/politics-government/article142732284.html#storylink=cpy

89. Ibid

90. http://www.sacbee.com/news/politics-government/article142732284.html

91. Ibid

92. https://www.washingtonpost.com/news/post-politics/wp/2013/04/04/obama-calls-kamala-harris-the-best-looking-attorney-general/?utm_term=.1b5f9fe38f73

93. https://www.campusreform.org/?ID=9179

94. Ibid

95. http://www.breitbart.com/california/2017/05/09/could-sen-kamala-harris-be-the-kryptonite-democrats-need-to-take-out-trump-in-2020/

96. http://calwatchdog.com/2013/04/07/why-kamala-harris-is-probably-not-thrilled-with-compliment/

97. http://articles.latimes.com/1994-11-29/news/mn-2787_1_brown-associates

98. Ibid

99. http://sfpoa.org/journal_archives/POAJournal_September2015.pdf

100. https://oag.ca.gov/sites/all/files/agweb/pdfs/cjsc/publications/homicide/hm08/preface.pdf

101. https://oag.ca.gov/sites/all/files/agweb/pdfs/cjsc/publications/homicide/hm08/preface.pdf

102. http://www.frontpagemag.com/fpm/259440/kathryn-steinles-fellow-victims-lloyd-billingsley

103. http://www.sfchronicle.com/crime/article/Pier-slaying-reveals-immigrant-justice-depends-on-6379649.php

104. http://www.washingtonexaminer.com/freshman-democrat-kamala-harris-grills-cia-director-nominee-on-climate-change/article/2611695

105. Ibid

106. Ibid

107. Ibid

108. http://www.pbs.org/newshour/bb/nancy-pelosi-offers-election-night-predictions/

109. Ibid

110. http://www.newsbusters.org/blogs/nb/kyle-drennen/2017/03/31/nbc-allows-nancy-pelosi-spin-conspiracy-theories-about-trump

111. Ibid

112. Ibid

113. https://pelosi.house.gov/biography/biography

114. http://www.theblaze.com/news/2017/03/28/watch-pelosi-heckled-by-liberal-protesters-during-town-hall-in-san-francisco/

115. https://www.usnews.com/news/articles/2017-03-24/obamacare-donald-trump-and-nancy-pelosis-potential-last-stand

116. Ibid

117. Ibid

118. http://www.breitbart.com/big-government/2017/06/24/maxine-waters-reacts-senate-health-bill-drag-trump-impeachment/

119. https://blackamericaweb.com/2017/04/16/maxine-waters-on-donald-trump-weve-got-to-stop-his-ass/

120. http://www.huffingtonpost.com/entry/maxine-waters-ben-carson_us_595a780de4b0da2c7324e375

121. Ibid

122. http://www.breitbart.com/big-government/2017/06/24/maxine-waters-reacts-senate-health-bill-drag-trump-impeachment/

123. https://www.citizensforethics.org/press-release/maxine-waters-named-most-corrupt-member-of-congress/

124. http://thehill.com/homenews/house/341677-house-dem-files-article-of-impeachment-against-trump

125. https://www.jihadwatch.org/2017/02/rep-brad-sherman-likens-trump-to-isis-says-both-bent-on-destroying-civilization

126. https://sherman.house.gov/media-center/press-releases/congressman-sherman-introduces-article-of-impeachment-obstruction-of

127. http://thehill.com/homenews/house/341677-house-dem-files-article-of-impeachment-against-trump

128. http://www.washingtonexaminer.com/rep-al-green-warns-of-more-articles-of-impeachment-against-trump/article/2628767

129. https://sherman.house.gov/media-center/press-releases/congressman-sherman-circulates-proposed-article-of-impeachment-0

130. http://www.washingtontimes.com/news/2017/jul/12/brad-sherman-california-democrat-launches-longshot/

131. http://www.cnn.com/2017/06/13/politics/house-democrats-impeachment-fight/index.html

132. http://www.foxnews.com/politics/2017/06/07/reps-green-and-sherman-announce-plan-to-file-articles-impeachment.html

133. http://www.nbcnews.com/politics/politics-news/schiff-defends-committee-examining-russia-trump-connections-n735391

134. http://www.newyorker.com/news/ryan-lizza/the-unlikely-liberal-hero-adam-schiff-is-ready-to-investigate-trump

135. http://ballotpedia.org/United_States_congressional_delegations_from_California

136. https://kevinmccarthy.house.gov/about

137. Ibid

138. http://www.breitbart.com/news/last-minute-bargaining-keyed-passage-of-gop-health-care-bill/

139. http://www.foxnews.com/politics/2017/04/06/nunes-steps-down-from-russia-trump-investigation.html

140. http://talkingpointsmemo.com/livewire/devin-nunes-russia-probe-protect-republicans

141. http://www.foxnews.com/politics/2017/04/06/nunes-steps-down-from-russia-trump-investigation.html

142. Ibid

143. http://www.foxnews.com/politics/2017/04/06/nunes-steps-down-from-russia-trump-investigation.html

144. http://talkingpointsmemo.com/livewire/devin-nunes-russia-probe-protect-republicans

145. Ibid

146. https://issa.house.gov/about/about-darrell

147. http://www.latimes.com/politics/la-pol-ca-richest-in-congress-darrell-issa-story.html

148. http://www.politico.com/story/2017/02/issa-trump-russia-probe-special-prosecutor-235387

149. http://hotair.com/archives/2016/11/29/ap-issa-finally-wins-house-race/

150. http://www.latimes.com/politics/essential/la-pol-ca-essential-politics-updates-another-democrat-jumps-into-the-2018-1489003574-htmlstory.html

151. http://sandiegofreepress.org/2017/02/nationwide-indivisible-movement-challenges-issa-elected-officials/

152. http://www.latimes.com/politics/essential/la-pol-ca-essential-politics-updates-rep-darrell-issa-calls-on-the-gop-to-1488063625-htmlstory.html

153. https://lamalfa.house.gov/about/full-biography

154. https://www.gop.gov/member/tom-mcclintock/

155. https://www.gop.gov/member/paul-cook/

156. https://www.gop.gov/member/jeff-denham/

157. https://www.gop.gov/member/david-valadao/

158. https://www.gop.gov/member/steve-knight/

159. https://www.gop.gov/member/ed-royce/

160. https://www.gop.gov/member/ken-calvert/

161. https://www.gop.gov/member/mimi-walters/

162. http://en.wikipedia.org/wiki/California%27s_45th_congressional_district

163. https://www.gop.gov/member/duncan-hunter-2/

164. http://www.sandiegouniontribune.com/news/politics/sd-me-hunter-race-20170522-story.html

165. https://www.gop.gov/member/dana-rohrabacher/

166. http://www.politico.com/story/2016/11/putin-congress-rohrabacher-trump-231775

167. https://www.newsreview.com/sacramento/sanctuary-in-sacramento-president-trumps/content?oid=23745258

168. http://calwatchdog.com/2013/07/10/mayor-steinberg-a-disaster-in-waiting-for-sacramento/

169. http://kfbk.iheart.com/articles/kfbk-news-461777/sacto-mayor-vows-to-fight-trump-15519019/#ixzz4go02iGXb

170. http://www.sacbee.com/news/local/article128760989.html

171. https://townhall.com/tipsheet/leahbarkoukis/2017/02/06/trump-threatens-to-defund-out-of-control-california-n2282007

172. http://www.sacbee.com/news/local/article148768194.html

173. http://canadafreepress.com/article/senator-steinbergs-liberal-indifference-to-waste-and-failure

174. http://www.sacbee.com/news/local/news-columns-blogs/marcos-breton/article136431968.html

175. Ibid

176. https://ww2.kqed.org/news/2017/01/26/mayor-ed-lee-reinforces-sanctuary-city-commitment/

177. http://www.sfexaminer.com/sf-sues-trump-sanctuary-city-executive-order/

178. Ibid

179. Ibid

180. Ibid

181. http://www.openthebooks.com/openthebooks_oversight_report_-_federal_funding_of_americas_sanctuary_cities/

182. Ibid

183. Ibid

184. Ibid

185. https://www.documentcloud.org/documents/3474587-022417-LALetter-ICE.html

186. http://opslens.com/2017/03/11/immigration-customs-enforcement-eric-garcetti-lapd/

187. https://ww2.kqed.org/news/2017/02/22/president-trump-could-be-biggest-hurdle-in-l-a-s-olympic-bid/

188. https://www.sandiego.gov/mayor/about/fullbio

189. http://www.sandiegouniontribune.com/news/politics/sd-me-faulconer-travel-20170131-story.html

190. http://www.sandiegouniontribune.com/news/politics/sd-me-faulconer-border-20170125-story.html

191. http://sandiegofreepress.org/2017/03/mayor-faulconer-says-no-to-trump-immigration-scheme/

192. http://fox5sandiego.com/2017/06/01/faulconer-denounces-trumps-move-to-pull-us-from-paris-climate-agreement/

193. http://www.latimes.com/politics/essential/la-pol-ca-essential-politics-updates-when-it-comes-to-trump-l-a-s-democrat-1479939346-htmlstory.html

194. http://www.nbcsandiego.com/news/local/Faulconer-No-Trump-No-Border-Wall-382324931.html

195. http://www.latimes.com/politics/essential/la-pol-ca-essential-politics-updates-san-diego-mayor-kevin-faulconer-says-he-1498861030-htmlstory.html

196. http://www.latimes.com/politics/la-pol-ca-california-legislature-eric-holder-donald-trump-20170104-story.html

197. https://www.nytimes.com/2017/01/04/us/california-eric-holder-donald-trump.html?_r=0

198. http://www.breitbart.com/california/2017/02/09/no-one-knows-eric-holder-california/

199. http://www.zerohedge.com/news/2017-01-04/california-dems-retain-eric-holder-fight-clear-and-present-danger-trump?page=1

200. http://www.washingtontimes.com/news/2017/jan/12/holder-hire-violates-calif-constitution-lawmaker/

201. Ibid

202. http://www.sacbee.com/news/politics-government/capitol-alert/article153825944.html

203. https://www.facebook.com/assemblymankiley

CHAPTER 2: CALIFORNIA'S ECONOMY: TAXED AND REGULATED
204. http://www.sacbee.com/news/business/article83780667.html

205. Ibid

206. http://abcnews.go.com/Politics/sunday-week-jeff-sessions-xavier-becerra/story?id=46945944

207. http://www.PolitiFact.com/california/statements/2016/jul/26/kevin-de-leon/does-california-really-have-sixth-largest-economy-/

208. Ibid

209. http://www.sacbee.com/news/politics-government/politics-columns-blogs/dan-walters/article101657302.html

210. https://www.census.gov/content/dam/Census/library/publications/2016/demo/p60-258.pdf

211. http://www.PolitiFact.com/california/statements/2017/jan/20/chad-mayes/true-california-has-nations-highest-poverty-rate-w/

212. http://abcnews.go.com/US/story?id=93303

213. http://time.com/4443382/donald-trump-economic-speech-detroit-transcript/

214. http://www.washingtontimes.com/news/2016/sep/15/obama-economic-policies-make-america-weak/

215. http://www.ppic.org/main/publication.asp?i=1230

216. http://www.bankrate.com/finance/taxes/state-taxes-california.aspx

217. https://taxfoundation.org/2017-tax-brackets/

218. https://taxfoundation.org/corporate-income-tax-rates-around-world-2015/

219. https://www.bloomberg.com/politics/articles/2016-12-26/democrats-plotting-collision-course-with-trump-s-tax-plan?mid=86407&rid=18816672

220. http://www.nysun.com/editorials/the-schwarzenegger-tax/83283/

221. http://www.sacbee.com/news/politics-government/politics-columns-blogs/dan-walters/article2589145.html

222. http://www.breitbart.com/california/2017/03/31/gov-jerry-brown-democrats-stick-it-to-working-poor-with-huge-tax-increase/

223. http://www.sacbee.com/news/politics-government/capitol-alert/article155169859.html

224. http://www.ocregister.com/2017/05/12/more-spending-little-restraint-in-new-budget/

225. http://www.latimes.com/politics/la-pol-sac-skelton-california-income-tax-reform-20170424-story.html

226. http://www.sacbee.com/news/politics-government/politics-columns-blogs/dan-walters/article37733694.html

227. http://www.latimes.com/local/california/la-me-lopez-environment-california-trump-0409-story.html

228. http://fortune.com/2015/04/13/death-tax-killing-american-family-farms/

229. https://www.forbes.com/sites/robertwood/2017/02/23/trump-vows-estate-tax-repeal-but-california-plans-its-own-40-estate-tax/#66c4790d1e2d

230. http://sd11.senate.ca.gov/news/20170221-senator-wiener-announces-ballot-measure-create-california-estate-tax-replace-federal

231. https://calmatters.org/articles/money-and-clout-on-the-line-for-teachers-union-in-2016/

232. http://reason.com/blog/2016/08/09/californias-six-figure-pension-club

233. http://www.sacbee.com/news/politics-government/politics-columns-blogs/dan-walters/article152923419.html

234. Ibid

235. Ibid

236. http://www.zerohedge.com/news/2016-12-02/stanford-study-reveals-california-pensions-underfunded-1-trillion-or-93k-household

237. https://www.mercatus.org/statefiscalrankings/california

238. https://www.whitehouse.gov/the-press-office/2017/01/24/
executive-order-expediting-environmental-reviews-and-approvals-
high?mid=84835&rid=18816672

239. http://www.cnn.com/2015/11/06/politics/keystone-xl-pipeline-
decision-rejection-kerry/

240. https://www.whitehouse.gov/the-press-office/2017/01/24/
presidential-memorandum-regarding-construction-dakota-access-
pipeline?mid=84835&rid=18816672

241. https://keystonepipeline-xl.state.gov/documents/organization/221135.
pdf?mid=84835&rid=18816672

242. http://www.energyxxi.org/sites/default/files/file-tool/Assessing_the_
Impact_of_Potential_New_Carbon_Regulations_in_the_United_
States.pdf?mid=84835&rid=18816672

243. https://ww2.kqed.org/news/2017/01/24/live-brown-delivers-
california-state-of-the-state-address/

244. http://usat.ly/2oTTHCr

245. https://news.usc.edu/97920/southern-californias-reduction-in-smog-
linked-to-major-improvement-in-childrens-respiratory-health/

246. Ibid

247. Ibid

248. Alan Lloyd, Power Point Presentation, 01/31/2014

249. http://www.sacbee.com/news/politics-government/capitol-alert/article144648379.html

250. Ibid

251. http://www.sandiegouniontribune.com/news/environment/sd-me-science-march-20170422-story.html

252. https://www.cato.org/publications/commentary/politicization-science-is-undermining-credibility-academia

253. http://www.reuters.com/article/us-usa-trump-autos-california-idUSKBN16M3DU?feedType=RSS&feedName=domesticNews

254. http://www.sacbee.com/news/politics-government/capitol-alert/article144648379.html

255. Ibid

256. http://www.capradio.org/articles/2017/05/15/california-business-group-revives-efforts-against-cap-and-trade-program/

257. http://www.latimes.com/politics/essential/la-pol-ca-essential-politics-updates-cap-and-trade-supreme-1498684764-htmlstory.html

258. http://www.latimes.com/politics/la-pol-sac-california-climate-policies-20170511-story.html

259. http://www.latimes.com/nation/la-na-pol-epa-confirmation-20170118-story.html?=

260. http://www.latimes.com/politics/essential/la-pol-ca-essential-politics-updates-california-s-waiver-appears-secure-for-1497547579-htmlstory.html

261. http://www.latimes.com/politics/essential/la-pol-ca-essential-politics-updates-1494361070-htmlstory.html

262. http://www.sacbee.com/news/politics-government/capitol-alert/article143456754.html

263. http://www.capitalpress.com/California/20161020/californias-multi-billion-dollar-nut-boom-keeps-going

264. http://digital.olivesoftware.com/Olive/ODN/SacBee/PrintArticle.aspx?doc=MSB%2F2017%2F04%2F06&entity=ar00115&mode=text

265. https://www.whitehouse.gov/the-press-office/2017/01/20/memorandum-heads-executive-departments-and-agencies?mid=84835&rid=18816672

266. https://www.whitehouse.gov/the-press-office/2017/01/30/presidential-executive-order-reducing-regulation-and-controlling?mid=84835&rid=18816672

267. http://www.baaqmd.gov/

268. http://www.sfgate.com/bayarea/article/Bay-Area-air-quality-agency-tackles-climate-change-11084992.php

269. Ibid In "Making roads friendlier for electric cars" it may be noted that even California agencies are in conflict, as the state in contrast raised taxes on owners of electric cars in 2017 as part of a new, $52 billion transportation tax program. http://www.greencarreports.com/news/1109824_even-california-imposes-new-fee-on-electric-cars-in-lieu-of-gas-taxes

270. http://www.cbsnews.com/news/california-climate-change-rules-on-cows-landfill-emissions/

271. http://www.ppic.org/main/publication.asp?i=1230

272. http://www.latimes.com/local/lanow/la-me-ln-santa-barbara-oil-spill-1969-20150520-htmlstory.html

273. http://www.ppic.org/main/publication_show.asp?i=1172

274. http://www.pewinternet.org/2016/10/04/the-politics-of-climate/

275. https://www.nytimes.com/2016/10/05/science/climate-change-poll-pew.html

276. http://www.pewinternet.org/2016/10/04/the-politics-of-climate/

277. https://www.usatoday.com/story/news/politics/2017/03/27/president-trumps-executive-order-undo-obamas-clean-power-plan-rule/99697594/

278. http://www.energyxxi.org/sites/default/files/file-tool/Assessing_the_Impact_of_Potential_New_Carbon_Regulations_in_the_United_States.pdf?mid=84835&rid=18816672

279. https://cei.org/content/legal-and-economic-case-against-paris-climate-treaty

280. http://fortune.com/2017/01/30/donald-trump-paris-agreement-climate-change-withdraw/

281. http://www.latimes.com/politics/la-me-pol-ca-climate-jerry-brown-doomsayer-20151210-story.html

282. https://ec.europa.eu/clima/policies/international/negotiations/paris_en

283. http://digital.olivesoftware.com/Olive/ODN/SanFranciscoChronicle/PrintArticle.aspx?doc=HSFC%2F2017%2F06%2F01&entity=ar00100

284. http://www.lomborg.com/press-release-research-reveals-negligible-impact-of-paris-climate-promises

285. Ibid

286. https://www.epa.gov/ghgemissions/global-greenhouse-gas-emissions-data#Country

287. http://www.carbontracker.org/what-does-the-us-china-climate-change-agreement-mean-in-practice-analytical-insights/

288. Ibid

289. Not to be outdone by China or the United States, Governor Brown signed his own executive order in 2015 establishing the steepest target of 40 percent reduction in emissions to below 1990 levels by 2030. https://www.gov.ca.gov/news.php?id=18938

290. http://www.latimes.com/world/asia/la-fg-china-dirty-energy-20170601-story.html

291. https://cei.org/content/legal-and-economic-case-against-paris-climate-treaty

292. Ibid

293. https://www.whitehouse.gov/the-press-office/2017/06/01/statement-president-trump-paris-climate-accord

294. http://www.latimes.com/politics/essential/la-pol-ca-essential-politics-updates-gov-jerry-brown-calls-for-1490734956-htmlstory.html

295. https://ww2.kqed.org/science/2016/12/12/if-trump-wont-can-california-sign-the-international-climate-treaty/

296. http://www.governing.com/topics/transportation-infrastructure/tns-trump-paris-climate-brown-states.html

297. http://usa.chinadaily.com.cn/epaper/2017-06/07/content_29651174.htm

298. http://www.sfchronicle.com/politics/article/For-struggling-Kern-Trump-means-hope-and-change-11043909.php

299. Ibid

300. Ibid

301. http://www.latimes.com/local/political/la-me-pc-california-senate-votes-to-ban-new-oil-drilling-off-santa-barbara-co-coast-20150603-story.html

302. https://data.bls.gov/timeseries/LNS14000000?mid=84613&rid=18816672

303. Ibid

304. http://www.reuters.com/article/us-usa-economy-idUSKBN15I0I1?mid=84613&rid=18816672

305. http://www.gallup.com/poll/205307/economic-confidence-index-record-high.aspx?mid=84613&rid=18816672

306. http://www.cnbc.com/2017/04/24/trumps-stock-market-gain-in-the-first-100-days-tops-reagan-and-most-other-republican-presidents.html

307. http://www.cnbc.com/2017/01/30/the-next-recession-now-appears-further-away-thanks-to-trump-economist-says.html

308. https://www.usatoday.com/story/money/2017/06/29/u-s-economic-growth-q-1-upgraded-1-4/438536001/

309. Chart, Bureau of Economic Analysis, Jim Sergent, USA Today

310. https://www.bloomberg.com/news/articles/2017-07-28/second-quarter-u-s-growth-rate-of-2-6-underscores-resilience

311. http://www.ppic.org/main/publication_show.asp?i=794

312. http://www.sacbee.com/site-services/databases/article147139109.html

313. http://www.pasadenastarnews.com/business/20160719/california-ranked-as-least-business-friendly-state-blows-past-all-others-in-job-creation

314. http://www.cnbc.com/2017/03/14/4-ways-silicon-valley-will-thrive-under-trump.html

315. http://www.cnbc.com/2017/03/17/silicon-valley-tech-talent-fleeing-to-seattle.html

316. http://www.bankrate.com/finance/taxes/state-with-no-income-tax-better-or-worse-1.aspx

317. http://www.capoliticalreview.com/top-stories/trump-nominee-threatens-to-shake-up-central-valley-water-status-quo/

318. http://www.sacbee.com/news/state/california/water-and-drought/article153617779.html

319. http://www.mcclatchydc.com/news/politics-government/white-house/article138948383.html

320. http://www.pasadenastarnews.com/business/20161206/good-news-about-a-trump-economy-californias-defense-industry-could-benefit&template=printart

CHAPTER 3: SANCTUARY CITIES IN A SANCTUARY STATE

321. http://thehill.com/blogs/floor-action/house/340137-house-passes-kates-law-and-crackdown-on-sanctuary-cities

322. Ibid

323. http://www.breitbart.com/california/2017/05/23/california-grapples-new-sanctuary-city-definition/

324. http://www.latimes.com/politics/essential/la-pol-ca-essential-politics-updates-california-leads-nine-states-in-filing-1498695881-htmlstory.html

325. http://www.latimes.com/local/lanow/la-me-ln-malibu-sanctuary-city-20170320-story.html

326. http://www.dailynews.com/government-and-politics/20170327/la-mayor-vows-to-fight-trump-administration-attempt-to-strip-sanctuary-city-funding&template=printart

327. http://www.politico.com/states/california/story/2017/03/with-sanctuary-cities-in-trumps-crosshairs-local-governments-craft-a-response-110692

328. http://www.dailynews.com/social-affairs/20161115/its-not-our-job-lapd-wont-enforce-federal-immigration-laws-chief-says

329. http://www.sbsun.com/social-affairs/20170321/port-airport-police-barred-from-enforcing-immigration-laws&template=printart

330. http://www.latimes.com/local/lanow/la-me-ln-california-police-immigration-enforcement-20170412-story.html

331. http://www.kpbs.org/news/2017/mar/17/san-diego-mayor-kevin-faulconer/

332. http://www.sandiegouniontribune.com/news/immigration/sd-me-ice-detainers-20170401-story.html

333. http://www.latimes.com/local/california/la-me-sanctuary-cities-respond-to-ag-threats-20170327-story.html

334. http://www.therecorder.com/printerfriendly/id=1202778073347

335. http://www.politico.com/states/california/story/2017/03/with-sanctuary-cities-in-trumps-crosshairs-local-governments-craft-a-response-110692

336. http://www.sandiegouniontribune.com/opinion/commentary/sd-utbg-sanctuary-cities-opposition-20170120-story.html

337. http://dailycaller.com/2017/04/21/top-california-lawmaker-says-threats-to-defund-sanctuary-cities-represent-white-supremacy/

338. https://www.law.cornell.edu/uscode/text/8/1373

339. http://www.breitbart.com/california/2017/05/23/california-grapples-new-sanctuary-city-definition/

340. http://www.latimes.com/politics/la-na-pol-trump-sanctuary-city-20170522-story.html

341. https://www.gpo.gov/fdsys/pkg/BILLS-115hr3003ih/pdf/BILLS-115hr3003ih.pdf

342. https://www.washingtonpost.com/news/the-fix/wp/2017/04/11/california-lawmakers-are-setting-up-a-sanctuary-state-and-daring-trump-to-stop-them-can-he/?utm_term=.cbaa348e5959

343. http://www.courthousenews.com/california-closer-creating-sanctuary-state/

344. http://www.sacbee.com/news/politics-government/capitol-alert/article142502974.html

345. http://www.latimes.com/politics/essential/la-pol-ca-essential-politics-updates-california-senate-leader-kevin-de-le-n-1490886824-htmlstory.html

346. Ibid

347. http://www.eccalifornian.com/article/anderson-takes-stand-against-senate-%E2%80%9Csanctuary%E2%80%9D-bill-saying-it-deports-more-dreamers-protect

348. https://www.washingtonpost.com/news/post-nation/wp/2017/03/17/california-chief-justice-to-ice-stop-stalking-immigrants-at-courthouses/?utm_term=.ca12ff116943

349. Ibid

350. https://www.nytimes.com/interactive/2017/03/31/us/sessions-kelly-letter.html?mcubz=3

351. http://www.latimes.com/politics/washington/la-na-essential-washington-updates-trump-administration-fires-back-at-1490973610-htmlstory.html

352. http://www.politico.com/states/california/story/2017/03/with-sanctuary-cities-in-trumps-crosshairs-local-governments-craft-a-response-110692

353. http://news.berkeley.edu/2015/09/04/igs-poll-californians-oppose-sanctuary-city-flexibility/

354. http://news.berkeley.edu/story_jump/new-igs-poll-shows-divergent-views-about-immigration/

355. https://gallery.mailchimp.com/d77c7ab2fffb03c109d588f05/files/14175f9f-1108-4a11-851d-43f6fa377d2b/Berkeley_IGS_Poll_2017_02_illegal_immigration.pdf

356. http://www.ppic.org/publication/california-voter-and-party-profiles/

357. https://www.nytimes.com/elections/results/california

358. http://elections.cdn.sos.ca.gov/sov/2016-general/sov/17-presidential-formatted.pdf

359. http://www.sfchronicle.com/bayarea/article/If-California-becomes-a-sanctuary-state-this-11060428.php

360. Ibid

361. Ibid

362. http://www.foxandhoundsdaily.com/2017/03/sb-54-makes-california-sanctuary-dangerous-criminals/

363. Ibid

364. http://www.kpbs.org/news/2017/mar/29/san-diego-area-mayors-organize-opposition-sanctuar/

365. http://www.sfchronicle.com/bayarea/article/Worried-about-Trump-BART-rethinks-11014316.php

CHAPTER 4: INFRASTRUCTURE WOES

366. https://www.gov.ca.gov/news.php?id=19669

367. http://www.mercurynews.com/2017/02/17/oroville-dam-what-made-the-spillway-collapse/

368. Ibid

369. http://www.sacbee.com/news/politics-government/capitol-alert/article140122603.html

370. http://thehill.com/policy/transportation/333202-five-things-we-know-about-trumps-infrastructure-plan

371. Ibid

372. http://thehill.com/policy/transportation/333202-five-things-we-know-about-trumps-infrastructure-plan

373. http://www.latimes.com/politics/essential/la-pol-ca-essential-politics-updates-california-submits-100-billion-in-1486590025-htmlstory.html

374. http://www.latimes.com/opinion/editorials/la-ed-road-funding-20170401-story.html

375. http://www.ocregister.com/2017/04/07/gov-browns-massive-52-billion-road-repair-bill-which-raises-gas-tax-is-approved/

376. Ibid

377. http://kfiam640.iheart.com/content/2017-06-09-more-than-half-of-californias-registered-voters-oppose-the-gas-tax/

378. http://www.mercurynews.com/2017/02/17/oroville-dam-what-made-the-spillway-collapse/

379. http://www.ocregister.com/2017/02/26/the-true-legacy-of-gov-jerry-brown/

380. Ibid

381. http://patbrowndocumentary.com/home/index.html

382. http://www.ocregister.com/2017/02/26/the-true-legacy-of-gov-jerry-brown/

383. http://www.gao.gov/assets/220/212748.pdf

384. Ibid

385. http://media.sacbee.com/smedia/2013/12/07/21/47/r1OuL.So.4.pdf

386. calwatchdog.com/2013/12/11/update-critics-charge-sfoakland-bay-bridge-still-unsafe/

387. http://www.restorethedelta.org/2016/07/05/rebutting-the-latest-fast-facts-from-delta-tunnels-backers/

388. https://ballotpedia.org/California_Proposition_9,_the_Peripheral_Canal_Act_(June_1982)

389. http://www.latimes.com/local/lanow/la-me-delta-tunnels-20170626-story.html

390. http://www.history.com/topics/los-angeles-aqueduct

391. Ibid

392. http://www.flashreport.org/blog/2014/09/15/food-or-fish-political-honesty-needed-in-ca-water-wars/

393. Ibid

394. http://www.water.ca.gov/waterconditions/background.cfm

395. http://agwaterstewards.org/practices/water_energy/

396. http://www.sacbee.com/news/state/california/water-and-drought/article46665960.html

397. http://watchdog.org/155106/last-year-california-built-dam-1959/

398. http://watchdog.org/247722/california-hates-water/

399. Ibid

400. http://www.nationalreview.com/article/416918/no-farmers-dont-use-80-percent-californias-water-devin-nunes

401. http://www.pbs.org/newshour/updates/president-trump-promised-california-farmers-start-opening-water-can/

402. Ibid

403. http://www.npr.org/sections/thetwo-way/2012/07/25/157381596/gov-brown-unveils-new-water-tunnel-plans-for-california

404. http://www.ocregister.com/2017/03/11/gov-brown-wont-give-up-on-the-future-of-his-1970s-youth/

405. http://www.cc-hsr.org/assets/pdf/stillnotinvestmentgrade.pdf

406. http://calwatchdog.com/2012/04/14/high-speed-rail-is-mission-impossible/

407. Ibid

408. Ibid

409. https://leginfo.legislature.ca.gov/faces/billNavClient.xhtml?bill_id=201320140AB66

410. Ibid

411. https://ad23.asmrc.org/press-release/17854

412. Ibid

413. http://www.lao.ca.gov/analysis/2012/transportation/high-speed-rail-041712.aspx

414. Ibid

415. http://environmentblog.ncpa.org/high-speed-rail-decision-rule-of-law-in-california/#sthash.ebeLsxRF.dpbs

416. Ibid

417. http://www.flashreport.org/blog/2014/03/24/bill-to-stop-high-speed-rail-in-its-tracks/

418. http://environmentblog.ncpa.org/high-speed-rail-decision-rule-of-law-in-california/#sthash.ebeLsxRF.dpbs

419. http://www.latimes.com/local/california/la-me-bullet-train-trump-20170206-story.html

420. http://thehill.com/homenews/state-watch/318324-california-gop-asks-trump-to-halt-high-speed-rail-grants

421. http://www.mercurynews.com/2017/05/22/federal-fta-grant-caltrain-electrification/

422. http://www.sacbee.com/news/politics-government/capitol-alert/article141127698.html

423. http://www.sfchronicle.com/nation/article/California-demands-that-feds-pay-for-firefighting-11275158.php

CHAPTER 5: CALIFORNIA'S EDUCATIONAL BATTLEGROUND

424. http://www.politifact.com/ohio/statements/2016/sep/21/donald-trump/trump-us-spends-more-almost-any-other-major-countr/

425. https://edsource.org/2017/teachers-mount-protests-against-trumps-education-agenda-and-to-protect-public-schools/575744

426. http://www.cosmopolitan.com/politics/a8580091/betsy-devos-trump-administration-education-secretary/

427. Ibid

428. http://blogs.edweek.org/edweek/charterschoice/2017/03/how_might_trump_create_a_federal_tax-credit_scholarship_program.html

429. https://www.americanprogress.org/issues/education/reports/2017/01/31/297695/president-trumps-education-plan-puts-students-and-schools-at-risk/

430. http://www.npr.org/sections/ed/2017/01/18/510417234/the-devos-hearing-in-their-own-words

431. https://www.usnews.com/opinion/knowledge-bank/articles/2017-01-26/betsy-devos-probe-on-michigan-charters-shows-need-for-education-debate

432. http://www.glep.org/

433. http://www.latimes.com/local/education/la-me-trump-vouchers-california-20161221-story.html

434. http://www.npr.org/sections/ed/2017/01/18/510417234/the-devos-hearing-in-their-own-words

435. http://www.ocregister.com/2017/02/13/teachers-unions-hysterical-over-betsy-devos-school-choice/

436. Ibid

437. http://www.utla.net/news/10000-stand-shield-our-schools

438. http://www.cnn.com/2017/02/07/politics/betsy-devos-senate-vote/index.html

439. http://www.cde.ca.gov/fg/fr/eb/

440. http://www.cde.ca.gov/eo/bo/tt/

441. https://edsource.org/2014/millions-pour-into-state-superintendents-race/67975

442. Ibid

443. http://www.sandiegouniontribune.com/news/education/sd-me-state-assures-20161110-story.html

444. Ibid

445. https://www.ice.gov/

446. http://www.cde.ca.gov/nr/ne/yr17/yr17rel03.asp

447. http://www.sacbee.com/news/local/education/article140663243.html

http://www.cde.ca.gov/nr/ne/yr17/yr17rel21.asp

448. http://www.smdailyjournal.com/articles/lnews/2017-01-13/educators-salute-state-school-spending-plan-browns-increased-proposal-pulls-state-closer-to-pre-recession-spending/1776425174241.html

449. http://www.smdailyjournal.com/articles/lnews/2017-01-13/educators-salute-state-school-spending-plan-browns-increased-proposal-pulls-state-closer-to-pre-recession-spending/1776425174241.html

450. http://www.fresnobee.com/news/local/education/article57319733.html

451. https://calmatters.org/articles/trump_california/education-news/

452. https://calmatters.org/articles/trump_california/education-news/

453. http://www.thereporter.com/article/NG/20170223/NEWS/170229889

454. https://calmatters.org/articles/trump_california/education-news/

455. Ibid

456. https://edsource.org/2017/california-would-lose-400-million-in-federal-k-12-education-funding-under-trump-budget/582370

457. https://edsource.org/2017/californias-top-education-official-joins-court-fight-to-stop-threat-of-fiscal-penalties-to-sanctuaries/579324

458. Ibid

459. http://dailycaller.com/2017/04/24/politicized-teachers-push-radical-leftist-agenda/

460. Author interview with Lance Izumi, Koret senior fellow in education studies and senior director of the Center for Education at the Pacific Research Institute.

461. Ibid

462. http://www.sandiegouniontribune.com/sdut-california-student-test-scores-common-core-2016aug24-story.html

463. http://www.dailynews.com/social-affairs/20150609/lausd-board-passes-plan-to-help-seniors-graduate

464. http://www.cnbc.com/2015/10/28/california-students-score-near-bottom-in-math-and-reading.html

465. http://www.breitbart.com/california/2014/07/27/at-84-489-california-teachers-are-highest-paid-in-america/

466. http://www.businessinsider.com/do-school-vouchers-work-2017-2

467. https://edsource.org/2017/majority-of-californians-polled-favor-school-vouchers/580456

468. https://www.cta.org/~/media/Documents/Issues%20%20Action/Ed%20Reform/Vouchers/Vouchers%20NEA.pdf?dmc=1&ts=201706 13T1127306849

469. https://ed.stanford.edu/news/evidence-fails-show-school-vouchers-improve-student-achievement-stanford-researcher-finds

470. https://www.nytimes.com/2017/02/23/upshot/dismal-results-from-vouchers-surprise-researchers-as-devos-era-begins.html?mcubz=0

471. https://academic.oup.com/qje/article-abstract/113/2/553/1915757/Private-School-Vouchers-and-Student-Achievement-An

472. http://www.nber.org/papers/w16056

473. https://edsource.org/2016/trump-school-voucher-plan-would-face-huge-obstacles-in-california/573691

474. http://repository.uchastings.edu/ca_ballot_props/1089/

475. https://ballotpedia.org/California_Proposition_38,_School_Vouchers_(2000)

476. http://www.sacbee.com/news/politics-government/capitol-alert/article57960523.html

477. https://edsource.org/2016/trump-school-voucher-plan-would-face-huge-obstacles-in-california/573691

478. http://www.uncommonschools.org/our-approach/faq-what-is-charter-school

479. https://edsource.org/2017/lausd-election-new-data-provide-momentum-for-charter-schools/582784

480. http://laschoolreport.com/reformers-sweep-lausd-school-board-elections/

481. Ibid

482. http://www.ocregister.com/2014/02/18/gloria-romero-charter-schools-surging-in-us-california/

483. Ibid

484. http://www.ccsa.org/understanding/numbers/

485. https://www.ed.gov/news/speeches/secretary-betsy-devos-prepared-remarks-national-association-public-charter-schools

486. https://www.ed.gov/news/speeches/secretary-betsy-devos-prepared-remarks-national-association-public-charter-schools

487. http://www.breitbart.com/big-government/2017/02/05/five-reasons-betsy-devos-nomination-education-chief-controversial/

488. http://www.corestandards.org/about-the-standards/

489. https://www.pacificresearch.org/article/the-reality-of-common-core-in-the-classroom/

490. https://www.pacificresearch.org/article/the-reality-of-common-core-in-the-classroom/

491. https://www.usnews.com/news/special-reports/a-guide-to-common-core/articles/2014/02/27/who-is-fighting-for-common-core

492. http://www.breitbart.com/big-government/2017/02/05/five-reasons-betsy-devos-nomination-education-chief-controversial/

493. https://www.usnews.com/news/special-reports/a-guide-to-common-core/articles/2014/02/27/who-is-fighting-against-common-core

494. http://www.mercurynews.com/2013/09/10/california-schools-could-lose-federal-funding-over-star-test-suspension/

495. https://truthinamericaneducation.com/federalized-education/devos-news-blackout-conservative-media-mimic-liberal-media/

496. https://www.washingtonpost.com/news/answer-sheet/wp/2017/04/24/betsy-devos-said-there-isnt-really-any-common-core-any-more-um-yes-there-is/?utm_term=.0e1470f33820

497. http://thehill.com/blogs/pundits-blog/education/317719-after-protests-and-riots-free-speech-is-mia-on-college-campuses

498. http://www.thegatewaypundit.com/2017/05/breaking-berkeley-mayor-told-local-police-stand-conservatives-get-pummeled-riots/

499. Ibid

500. http://www.thegatewaypundit.com/2017/04/berkeley-mayor-publicly-supports-violent-antifa-group-blames-conservatives-citys-violent-clashes/

501. http://sanfrancisco.cbslocal.com/2017/02/02/police-tactics-during-violent-uc-berkeley-protest-questioned/

502. http://www.thegatewaypundit.com/2017/05/breaking-berkeley-mayor-told-local-police-stand-conservatives-get-pummeled-riots/

503. http://thefederalist.com/2017/04/28/berkeley-refuses-prevent-rioting-ann-coulter-speech-conservative-students-stand/

504. Ibid

505. http://www.yaf.org/news/statement-young-americas-foundations-april-27-lecture-uc-berkeley/

506. http://twitter.com/realDonaldTrump?ref_src=twsrc%5Etfw&ref_url=http%3A%2F%2Fthehill.com%2Fblogs%2Fpundits-blog%2Feducation%2F317719-after-protests-and-riots-free-speech-is-mia-on-college-campuses

507. https://calisphere.org/exhibitions/43/the-free-speech-movement/

508. https://www.auditor.ca.gov/pdfs/reports/2016-130.pdf

509. Ibid

510. http://www.dailydemocrat.com/article/NI/20170509/LOCAL1/170509858

511. https://patriotpost.us/commentary/19229

512. Ibid

513. http://www.foxnews.com/us/2017/05/30/university-california-to-end-lavish-spending-on-dinners.html

514. Ibid

515. http://www.bamn.com/trumpmustgo

516. http://eagnews.org/middle-school-teacher-with-history-of-instigating-violence-plays-key-role-in-berkeley-riot/

517. https://www.aft.org/news/trumps-budget-takes-meat-cleaver-public-education

518. http://m.washingtontimes.com/news/2017/mar/17/3-things-trumps-education-spending-plan/

519. http://www.capoliticalreview.com/capoliticalnewsandviews/grimes-dubious-deal-between-los-angeles-school-district-and-seiu/

520. Ibid

521. http://www.cde.ca.gov/fg/aa/lc/lcfffaq.asp

522. https://www.pacificresearch.org/article/key-brown-education-legacy-program-comes-up-short/

523. Author interview with Lance Izumi, Koret senior fellow in education studies and senior director of the Center for Education at the Pacific Research Institute.

524. Ibid

Chapter 6: California's Dangerous Medicare Expansion under Obamacare

525. http://www.sbsun.com/government-and-politics/20170519/as-dc-attacks-obamacare-california-takes-steps-toward-single-payer-healthcare

526. http://www.sacbee.com/opinion/op-ed/soapbox/article148488219.html

527. http://www.sbsun.com/government-and-politics/20170519/as-dc-attacks-obamacare-california-takes-steps-toward-single-payer-healthcare

528. http://www.sacbee.com/news/politics-government/capitol-alert/article151397597.html

529. Ibid

530. http://www.PolitiFact.com/california/article/2017/jul/07/fact-checking-claims-sens-kamala-harris-and-dianne/

531. http://www.sfchronicle.com/opinion/article/The-good-the-bad-and-the-ugly-of-Obamacare-10856843.php

532. http://www.sacbee.com/news/local/health-and-medicine/article2581742.html

533. http://www.sacbee.com/news/local/health-and-medicine/article152226372.html

534. Ibid

535. Ibid

536. http://www.latimes.com/opinion/op-ed/la-oe-gorman-medi-cal-obamacare-california-20140812-story.html

537. Ibid

538. Ibid

539. http://www.latimes.com/opinion/editorials/la-ed-la-county-ahca-20170627-story.html

540. Ibid

541. http://www.nationalreview.com/article/449126/california-medicaid-unsustainable-costs

542. http://www.PolitiFact.com/california/statements/2017/jan/20/chad-mayes/true-california-has-nations-highest-poverty-rate-w/

543. https://www.census.gov/quickfacts/fact/table/KS/PST045216

544. http://www.nationalreview.com/article/449126/california-medicaid-unsustainable-costs

545. https://aspe.hhs.gov/pdf-report/individual-market-premium-changes-2013-2017?mid=86980&rid=18816672

546. http://enewspaper.latimes.com/desktop/latimes/default.aspx?pubid=50435180-e58e-48b5-8e0c-236bf740270e

547. Ibid

548. Ibid

549. http://digital.olivesoftware.com/Olive/ODN/SacBee/PrintArticle.aspx?doc=MSB%2F2017%2F05%2F23&entity=ar00109&mode=text

CHAPTER 7: REAL RISKS TO HOMELAND SECURITY IN CALIFORNIA

550. https://www.fbi.gov/news/stories/fbi-will-investigate-san-bernardino-shootings-as-terrorist-act

551. https://www.fbi.gov/news/stories/fbi-will-investigate-san-bernardino-shootings-as-terrorist-act

552. https://www.fbi.gov/news/stories/fbi-will-investigate-san-bernardino-shootings-as-terrorist-act

553. http://www.latimes.com/nation/la-na-malik-visa-application-20151222-story.html

554. Ibid

555. Ibid

556. Ibid

557. http://www.sbsun.com/general-news/20161127/everything-we-know-about-the-san-bernardino-terror-attack-investigation

558. http://english.alarabiya.net/en/News/world/2015/12/05/FBI-investigating-California-massacre-as-act-of-terrorism-.html

559. http://www.latimes.com/local/lanow/la-me-san-bernardino-terror-probe-20161130-story.html

560. Ibid

561. http://time.com/4101903/climate-change-national-security/

562. https://www.gov.ca.gov/docs/GOV_MIL_REPORT_June.pdf

563. Ibid

564. https://www.fbi.gov/news/stories/fbi-will-investigate-san-bernardino-shootings-as-terrorist-act

565. http://www.latimes.com/local/lanow/la-me-terror-threat-transit-20161205-story.html

566. Ibid

567. https://www.theguardian.com/world/2017/apr/18/fresno-shooting-three-killed-california

568. http://www.foxnews.com/us/2017/04/19/ap-translates-fresno-shooters-allahu-akbar-to-god-is-great.html

569. Ibid

570. Ibid

571. http://www.mercurynews.com/2017/04/21/california-gunman-to-appear-in-court-on-murder-count/

572. http://www.dailymail.co.uk/news/article-4422714/1-killed-2-hurt-shooting-downtown-Fresno-California.html#ixzz4mTad8yuU

573. https://www.theguardian.com/world/2017/apr/18/fresno-shooting-three-killed-california

574. http://www.mercurynews.com/2017/04/21/california-gunman-to-appear-in-court-on-murder-count/

575. Ibid

576. Ibid

577. http://justice.gov/opa/pr/2007/September/07_nsd_700.html

578. http://www.nytimes.com/2007/09/11/us/11lodi.html

579. http://www.sandiegouniontribune.com/sdut-region-terrorist-cell-was-embedded-deeply-in-san-2011sep10-story.html

580. Ibid

581. https://www.usnews.com/news/articles/2016-09-23/is-the-energy-grid-in-danger

582. https://blogs.wsj.com/corporate-intelligence/2014/02/05/qa-what-you-need-to-know-about-attacks-on-the-u-s-power-grid/

583. Ibid

584. http://money.cnn.com/2015/10/16/technology/sniper-power-grid/index.html

585. https://blogs.wsj.com/corporate-intelligence/2014/02/05/qa-what-you-need-to-know-about-attacks-on-the-u-s-power-grid/

586. https://blogs.wsj.com/corporate-intelligence/2014/02/05/qa-what-you-need-to-know-about-attacks-on-the-u-s-power-grid/

587. Ibid

588. http://www.foxnews.com/us/2017/03/03/san-franciscos-withdrawal-from-national-terror-intelligence-network-hikes-risks-officials-say.html

589. Ibid

590. http://www.latimes.com/politics/la-pol-sac-jerry-brown-china-trip-20170601-story.html

591. http://www.breitbart.com/california/2017/06/07/jerry-brown-plays-president-signs-climate-deal-china/

592. http://www.heritage.org/constitution/#!/articles/1/essays/69/state-treaties

593. https://www.gov.ca.gov/news.php?id=19669

594. http://www.mercurynews.com/2017/07/06/jerry-brown-one-ups-trump-on-climate-change-with-g20-announcement/

595. Ibid

596. http://www.ocregister.com/2017/03/26/gov-brown-swipes-trump-for-border-wall-says-california-to-fight/

597. http://www.nbcbayarea.com/news/california/Gov-Brown-on-Meet-the-Press-You-Dont-Want-to-Mess-With-California-417239443.html

598. http://www.ocregister.com/2017/03/26/gov-brown-swipes-trump-for-border-wall-says-california-to-fight/

599. https://www.whitehouse.gov/briefing-room/nominations-and-appointments

600. http://www.cbc.ca/news/technology/cyberwarfare-donald-trump-us-president-foreign-policy-isis-1.3944993

601. https://www.whitehouse.gov/the-press-office/2017/06/15/background-briefing-presidents-cuba-policy

602. http://www.climatedepot.com/2017/01/17/danish-statistician-un-climate-treaty-will-cost-100-trillion-to-postpone-global-warming-by-less-than-four-year-by-2100/

Chapter 8: Whose Travel Ban?

603. http://www.cnbc.com/2017/01/30/trump-defends-his-immigration-ban-amid-uncertainty-public-outcry.html

604. http://www.laweekly.com/news/california-us-senator-attempts-to-overturn-so-called-muslim-ban-7879259

605. https://supreme.justia.com/cases/federal/us/582/15-1191/

606. Ibid

607. http://www.therecorder.com/printerfriendly/id=1202778575308

608. Ibid

609. http://www.latimes.com/local/lanow/la-na-9thcircuit-travel-ban-20170530-story.html

610. http://www.sfgate.com/nation/article/Trump-s-travel-ban-faces-crucial-test-in-11130839.php

611. http://enewspaper.latimes.com/desktop/latimes/default.aspx?pubid=50435180-e58e-48b5-8e0c-236bf740270e

612. http://www.sacbee.com/news/politics-government/capitol-alert/article141092843.html

613. Ibid

614. http://www.reuters.com/article/us-usa-trump-attorneygenerals-idUSKBN15D0XZ

615. https://realclearpolitics.com/elections/live_results/2016_general/president/map.html

616. Ibid

617. https://oag.ca.gov/news/press-releases/attorney-general-becerra-court-slaps-down-trump%E2%80%99s-travel-ban-once-again

618. https://oag.ca.gov/news/press-releases/attorney-general-becerra-high-court-will-determine-if-oval-office-can-trump

619. http://www.mercurynews.com/2017/03/22/report-californians-oppose-trumps-travel-ban-and-border-wall-but-want-immigrants-to-stay/

620. http://www.latimes.com/politics/essential/la-pol-ca-essential-politics-updates-cal-atty-gen-becerra-expands-travel-1498167813-htmlstory.html

621. Ibid

622. http://www.mercurynews.com/2017/06/22/california-has-a-travel-ban-8-states-including-texas-are-now-on-the-list/

623. http://sanfrancisco.cbslocal.com/2017/06/27/kentucky-mayors-exemption-california-lgbt-travel-ban/

624. http://www.kentucky.com/news/local/counties/fayette-county/article158967444.html

625. http://www.mercurynews.com/2017/06/22/california-has-a-travel-ban-8-states-including-texas-are-now-on-the-list/

626. https://www.usnews.com/news/best-states/california/articles/2017-06-22/california-ag-bans-state-travel-to-texas-3-other-states

627. Ibid

CHAPTER 9: THE WALL AND IMMIGRATION POLICY

628. http://www.gao.gov/products/GAO-17-331

629. http://www.cnbc.com/2017/05/30/donald-trumps-border-wall-a-progress-report.html

630. http://www.nationaleconomicseditorial.com/2017/02/21/costs-illegal-immigration-california/

631. http://www.pewresearch.org/fact-tank/2017/04/27/5-facts-about-illegal-immigration-in-the-u-s/

632. http://www.foxnews.com/us/2015/09/16/crime-wave-elusive-data-shows-frightening-toll-illegal-immigrant-criminals.html

633. http://www.PolitiFact.com/texas/statements/2016/sep/02/sean-hannity/sean-hannity-says-illegal-immigrants-account-75-pe/

634. https://en.wikipedia.org/wiki/Shooting_of_Kathryn_Steinle

635. http://www.cnn.com/2015/07/03/politics/trump-san-francisco-killing/

636. Ibid

637. http://kron4.com/2016/07/21/trump-mentions-kate-steinle-during-speech/

638. http://www.huffingtonpost.com/entry/donald-trumps-border-wall-an-annotated-timeline_us_58b5f363e4b02f3f81e44d7b

639. http://www.pbs.org/newshour/updates/donald-trumps-10-point-immigration-plan/

640. http://www.cnbc.com/2016/02/08/mexico-wont-pay-single-cent-for-trumps-stupid-wall.html

641. https://www.washingtonpost.com/opinions/mexico-will-pay-for-that-wall----eventually/2017/01/08/64632e36-d44e-11e6-9cb0-54ab630851e8_story.html?utm_term=.ff90915f4488

642. http://www.sacbee.com/news/politics-government/politics-columns-blogs/dan-walters/article142032079.html

643. Ibid

644. http://www.sandiegouniontribune.com/business/economy/sd-fi-trump-border-wall-otay-mesa-20170424-story.html

645. Ibid

646. http://www.sandiegouniontribune.com/business/economy/sd-fi-border-wal-20170404-story.html

647. http://dailysignal.com//print?post_id=327588

648. Ibid

649. Ibid

650. http://www.sandiegouniontribune.com/news/immigration/sd-me-border-visit-20170421-story.html

651. http://digital.olivesoftware.com/Olive/ODN/SacBee/PrintArticle.aspx?doc=MSB%2F2017%2F04%2F24&entity=ar00503&mode=text

652. Ibid

653. http://www.washingtonexaminer.com/border-apprehensions-hit-17-year-low-in-march/article/2619338?mid=84766&rid=18816672

654. https://www.washingtonpost.com/news/fact-checker/wp/2017/04/11/president-trumps-claim-that-illegal-immigration-is-down-64-

percent-because-of-his-administration/?mid=84766&rid=18816672&
utm_term=.231b7f940045

655. http://www.reuters.com/article/us-usa-immigration-mothers-insight-
idUSKBN17F23M?utm_source=Twitter&utm_medium=Social&mid=
84766&rid=18816672

656. https://www.washingtonpost.com/local/immigration-arrests-
of-noncriminals-double-under-trump/2017/04/16/98a2f1e2-
2096-11e7-be2a-3a1fb24d4671_story.html?mid=84766&rid=
18816672&utm_term=.5f7b2ec87ffd

657. http://www.sandiegouniontribune.com/news/public-safety/sd-me-dui-
deportee-20170509-story.html

658. http://www.mercurynews.com/2016/11/18/trump-and-immigrants-
wide-fear-of-deportations-in-region/

659. http://www.dailynews.com/general-news/20170525/ice-arrests-nearly-
190-immigrants-in-southern-california-including-convicted-rapist

660. http://www.dailynews.com/article/20170405/NEWS/170409710&tem
plate=printart

661. Ibid

662. http://www.salon.com/2017/04/16/slow-motion-collision-course-
california-trumps-feds-headed-to-major-clash-on-immigration_
partner/

663. http://www.sandiegouniontribune.com/business/economy/sd-fi-sb30-
trump-20170406-story.html

664. Ibid

665. http://www.sfchronicle.com/politics/article/2-SF-supes-seek-to-punish-companies-for-bidding-11015709.php

666. http://www.dailynews.com/government-and-politics/20170509/helping-to-build-trumps-wall-an-la-leader-wants-the-public-to-know

667. http://www.sandiegouniontribune.com/business/economy/sd-fi-sb30-trump-20170406-story.html

668. http://www.dailynews.com/government-and-politics/20170407/mexican-governors-slam-trumps-offensive-border-wall-at-la-city-hall

669. http://www.politico.com/story/2017/03/jerry-brown-border-wall-trump-236494

670. http://www.sandiegouniontribune.com/news/environment/sd-me-wall-lawsuit-20170412-story.html

671. Ibid

672. http://www.latimes.com/local/lanow/la-me-ln-la-justice-fund-20170417-story.html

673. http://www.latimes.com/politics/la-pol-ca-immigrant-defense-state-budget-20170514-story.html

674. http://www.latimes.com/local/lanow/la-me-ln-ice-detainer-request-list-20170320-story.html

675. http://www.mercurynews.com/2017/03/21/santa-clara-alameda-counties-on-ice-shame-list-of-those-not-detaining-immigrants/

676. http://www.corpcounsel.com/printerfriendly/id=1202782851650

677. ttp://www.therecorder.com/printerfriendly/id=1202783998014

678. http://www.corpcounsel.com/printerfriendly/id=1202782851650

679. Ibid

680. http://digital.olivesoftware.com/Olive/ODN/SanFranciscoChronicle/
PrintArticle.aspx?doc=HSFC%2F2017%2F04%2F10&entity
=ar00105

681. Ibid

682. Ibid

683. http://www.sfchronicle.com/business/article/H-1B-visa-applications-
drop-for-first-time-in-11078751.php

684. http://www.breitbart.com/california/2015/07/18/more-than-
half-of-new-ca-drivers-licenses-go-to-illegal-immigrants/

685. http://www.scpr.org/blogs/multiamerican/2013/10/03/14885/
undocumented-immigrants-to-legally-obtain-driver-s/

686. https://leginfo.legislature.ca.gov/faces/billNavClient.
xhtml?bill_id=201320140AB60

687. http://www.mercurynews.com/2016/12/28/dmv-licensed-800000-
undocumented-immigrants-under-2-year-old-law/

688. http://thehill.com/blogs/pundits-blog/immigration/221914-drivers-
licenses-for-illegal-immigrants-an-issues-in-three

689. http://www.routefifty.com/2016/12/california-immigrant-
data-feds/133799/

690. Ibid

691. Author interview with confidential DMV informant.

692. https://calmatters.org/articles/if-feds-try-to-id-deportable-immigrants-using-cal-data-state-will-block-access/

693. http://sd33.senate.ca.gov/news/2015-10-09-governor-signs-lara%E2%80%99s-health-all-kids-act

694. http://californiahealthline.org/morning-breakout/new-law-will-expand-medical-to-170k-undocumented-children/

695. http://sd33.senate.ca.gov/health4all

696. http://sd33.senate.ca.gov/health4all

697. http://www.dhcs.ca.gov/services/medi-cal/eligibility/Pages/Medi-CalFAQs2014b.aspx

698. http://www.pbs.org/newshour/rundown/how-undocumented-immigrants-sometimes-receive-medicaid-treatment/

699. http://www.dhcs.ca.gov/services/medi-cal/eligibility/Pages/Medi-CalFAQs2014b.aspx

700. https://californiafoodstamps.org/Callfresh

701. http://www.christianpost.com/news/is-illegal-immigration-no-longer-a-crime-in-california-142657/

702. http://www.nationaleconomicseditorial.com/2017/02/21/costs-illegal-immigration-california/

703. http://www.christianpost.com/news/is-illegal-immigration-no-longer-a-crime-in-california-142657/

704. Ibid

705. http://www.capoliticalreview.com/capoliticalnewsandviews/antonovich-the-economic-and-human-toll-of-illegal-immigration/

CHAPTER 10: RISING CRIME IN CALIFORNIA

706. https://pjmedia.com/trending/2017/02/24/crime-increasing-in-california-after-prison-reform/

707. https://www.washingtonpost.com/news/post-nation/wp/2017/02/09/in-executive-actions-president-trump-vows-crackdown-on-violent-crime-is-america-as-unsafe-as-he-thinks/?utm_term=.45271731a404

708. http://www.cdcr.ca.gov/realignment/

709. https://ballotpedia.org/California_Proposition_47,_Reduced_Penalties_for_Some_Crimes_Initiative_(2014)

710. https://ballotpedia.org/California_Proposition_57,_Parole_for_Non-Violent_Criminals_and_Juvenile_Court_Trial_Requirements_(2016)

711. Ibid

712. https://pjmedia.com/trending/2017/02/24/crime-increasing-in-california-after-prison-reform/

713. https://www.amazon.com/Taxifornia-2016-Essays-Future-California/dp/0692450181

714. Ibid

715. Ibid

716. http://ktla.com/2017/02/21/man-suspected-of-killing-whittier-police-officer-and-cousin-to-be-identified-tuesday-afternoon-lasd/

717. http://www.allgov.com/usa/ca/departments/independent-agencies/department_of_corrections_and_rehabilitation?agencyid=223

718. http://reaganbabe.com/2016/10/gov-jerry-brown-and-democrats-undermining-law-and-order-dismantling-california/

719. http://www.foxnews.com/us/2017/04/17/did-california-prison-reform-lead-to-increase-in-crime.html

720. http://www.latimes.com/local/lanow/la-me-crime-stats-20161227-story.html

721. http://www.sfchronicle.com/crime/article/S-F-car-break-ins-up-31-percent-nearly-triple-6894503.php

722. Ibid

723. http://www.sfchronicle.com/bayarea/article/Richmond-mayor-witnessed-mob-attack-outside-BART-11305657.php

724. http://sanfrancisco.cbslocal.com/2017/07/09/bart-withholding-surveillance-videos-of-crime-to-avoid-stereotypes/

725. https://www.forbes.com/pictures/mlj45jggj/3-oakland/#3c75fc4e7d73

726. Ibid

727. http://www.sacbee.com/news/politics-government/politics-columns-blogs/dan-walters/article105521141.html

728. Ibid

729. http://www.politifact.com/california/statements/2017/mar/06/jeff-stone/has-violent-crime-been-rise-california-2011-and-di/

730. https://calmatters.org/articles/charticle-californias-crime-on-the-rise/

731. https://www.city-journal.org/html/illegal-alien-crime-wave-12492.html

732. http://www.cnn.com/2017/02/09/politics/trump-executive-orders-crime-reduction/index.html

733. Ibid

734. https://www.justice.gov/opa/pr/department-justice-sends-letter-nine-jurisdictions-requiring-proof-compliance-8-usc-1373

735. Ibid

736. https://www.justice.gov/opa/pr/department-justice-sends-letter-nine-jurisdictions-requiring-proof-compliance-8-usc-1373

737. Ibid

738. https://www.dhs.gov/news/2017/02/21/qa-dhs-implementation-executive-order-border-security-and-immigration-enforcement

739. http://abcnews.go.com/amp/Politics/wireStory/justice-dept-tells-sanctuary-cities-grant-money-risk-46938346

740. http://sd24.senate.ca.gov/news/2017-04-21-statement-california-senate-leader-us-attorney-general-request

741. http://www.gao.gov/products/GAO-11-187

742. Ibid

743. http://www.dailywire.com/news/9521/report-crime-spikes-sanctuary-cities-hank-berrien

744. http://www.nationalreview.com/article/421286/immigration-boon-democrats-ian-smith

745. http://sd24.senate.ca.gov/news/2017-04-21-statement-california-senate-leader-us-attorney-general-request

FOR MORE INFORMATION:

Visit James V. Lacy's author page at Amazon:
www.Amazon.com/author/james.lacy

Visit *Taxifornia*'s Facebook page at
https://www.facebook.com/taxifornia.book

Visit and subscribe to the daily e-mail newsletter at
California Political Review at:
www.capoliticalreview.com

Follow James V. Lacy on Twitter @JamesVLacy1

• • •

Visit Katy Grimes's website,
KATY GRIMES Sang-Froid Conservative:
https://sacramentocitizen.wordpress.com/

Visit Katy Grimes's Facebook page:
https://www.facebook.com/katygrimes?ref=tn_tnmn

Follow Katy Grimes on Twitter @KATYSaccitizen

Made in the USA
San Bernardino, CA
13 September 2017